HERE
THERE BE
WITCHES

Jane Yolen

HERE THERE BE WITCHES

Illustrated by DAVID WILGUS

HARCOURT BRACE & COMPANY

San Diego   New York   London

Requests for permission to make copies of any part of the work
should be mailed to: Permissions Department, Harcourt Brace & Company,
6277 Sea Harbor Drive, Orlando, Florida 32887-6777.

"The Magic House" previously appeared in *Best Witches* by Jane Yolen, copyright © 1989 by
Jane Yolen, published by G. P. Putnam's Sons. "Boris Chernevsky's Hands" by Jane Yolen
previously appeared in *Hecate's Cauldron*, edited by Susan Schwartz, copyright © 1982 by Jane
Yolen, published by DAW. "Witch's Cat" by Jane Yolen first appeared in *Ragged Shadows*, edited
by Lee Bennett Hopkins, copyright © 1992 by Jane Yolen, published by Little, Brown. "The
Face in the Cloth" by Jane Yolen first appeared in the *Magazine of Fantasy and Science Fiction*,
copyright © 1985 by Jane Yolen. "The Promise" previously appeared in *The Hundredth Dove* by
Jane Yolen, copyright © 1977 by Jane Yolen, published by T. Y. Crowell. "Circles" by Jane
Yolen first appeared in *Witch Fantastic*, edited by Mike Resnick, copyright © 1995 by Jane
Yolen, published by DAW. "The Woman Who Loved a Bear" by Jane Yolen previously
appeared in *Tales from the Great Turtle*, edited by Piers Anthony and Richard Gilliam, copyright
© 1994 by Jane Yolen, published by Tor Books. "The Sword and the Stone" previously
appeared in *Merlin's Booke* by Jane Yolen, copyright © 1985 by Jane Yolen, published by Ace
Books. All reprinted by permission of the author's agent, Curtis Brown, Ltd.

Library of Congress Cataloging-in-Publication Data
Yolen, Jane.
Here there be witches/by Jane Yolen; illustrated by David Wilgus.—1st ed.
p.   cm.
Summary: Presents an illustrated collection of seventeen stories
and poems about witches, wizards, and warlocks.
ISBN 0-15-200311-8
1. Witches—Literary collections.   2. Wizards—Literary collections.
3. Magic—Literary collections.   [1. Witches—Literary collections.
2. Wizards—Literary collections.   3. Magic—Literary collections.]
I. Wilgus, David, ill.   II. Title.
PZ7.Y78Hm   1995   [Fic]—dc20   94-37082

Designed by Camilla Filancia
First edition   A B C D E

Printed in the United States of America

To my wonderful editor

L I Z   B I C K N E L L

and for her children

Contents

HERE
THERE BE
WITCHES

Think of a witch story and you think of Hansel and Gretel. Or at least I do.
It probably goes back to junior high. I went to an all-girls school and we put
on a production of Humperdinck's fairy opera. I played Hansel because I had
the deepest voice in the class, a low alto. The class soprano, Pat Adel, played
Gretel, even though she was about a foot taller than I. We were a great success.

The Magic House

We should have known when we tasted the eaves,
Breaking them off like toffee
And cramming them into our mouths.
And the dear little windows, the color of coffee,
And chocolate doorknobs,
And windowpanes striped with mint.
We should have guessed at the chimney smoke,
White marshmallow fluff.
Taken the hint
From the marzipan bricks
And the fence posts made of bone rubble.
But it was only when we saw the witch
That we knew we were in deep, deep trouble.

In Katherine M. Briggs's book Pale Hecate's Team *is a passage from one of the accounts of witchcraft trials: "This Agnes Browne led her life at Gilsborough in the County of Northampton, of poor parentage and poor education, one that as shee was borne to no good, was for want of grace neuer in the way to receiu any, euer noted to bee of an ill nature and wicked disposition, spightfull and malitious . . ." She was executed as a witch in Northampton, England, in 1612.*

Initially I was attracted to that passage because of its wonderful archaic spellings and the mention of Northampton. I live next door to Northampton, Massachusetts. But as I read it over, an opening for a story of my own began. I grafted that bit of real history onto an old folktale that I had read long ago about a man who was ridden like a horse by his witch wife.

I began writing the story on a lovely Scottish summer day, having just come back from the St. Andrews Lammas Fair. The fair, a tradition in the town, going back to A.D. 1153, takes place on Market and South Streets. But another two streets over is Witch's Hill, where a different sort of tradition is remembered. There, in the seventeenth century, women believed to be witches were tortured, then burned to death. They were mostly old women, ugly women, often "spightfull" women who could not withstand their neighbors' accusations or the witchhunters' hideous methods of torture. Such things would never happen today. Would they?

The Witch's Ride

Agnes Browne lived in Gilsborough in the County of Northampton, of poor parentage and poorer education. She was born to no good, her neighbors said, never in the way of receiving any grace, nor wanting it. She was spiteful, they said, and malicious. Ugly, too. So they called her a witch, though she wasn't one.

Emily Early also lived in Gilsborough, and a blithe-looking girl was she. Always smiling and laughing, as if every living thing told her an amusing tale. She had golden hair and a golden disposition and if ever grace shone on a spirit, it was on hers, or so said her neighbors. But unbeknownst to them, Emily Early was a witch and she practiced her dark arts secretly and alone.

Now, one day in summer two black cats wandered through the streets of Gilsborough, yowling and howling as if looking for trouble. They fetched up by Agnes Browne's rude cottage and sat there for a while, preening one another and passing the time. Anon they set off again, once more yowling.

It was right after this that Mistress Goody's baby daughter, Charity, went missing. The milk curdled in Mistress Dwight's churn. Three black crows flew west over Squire Danforth's field and immediately his prize bull escaped from its meadow.

A crowd gathered quickly at Agnes Browne's door, where so recently the two black cats had been seen gossiping. A mob reasons with rumor. They called Agnes forth, trampled her flowers, and pulled the latch from her door.

She came out, her spiteful tongue wagging. "Clear off my stoop and out of my yard, you ill-bred ninnywits!" It did not help her cause that she spat as she spoke.

They bound her tight with the binding of the three narrows: wrists, elbows, knees. Then they dragged her to Witch's Hill, a place of dreadful inquiry. And there, though Squire Danforth's bull was soon caught, though Mistress Goody's Charity was found in the henhouse cracking eggs, there they named poor Agnes Browne a witch. Three witch-hunters were brought in from London to question her and at last she confessed. She said that the two cats were not cats at all but familiar spirits named Bobbin and Drew. And having confessed, she was given a quick death, too quick for her to repent, but not so quick that she could not call down a curse on them all.

3

"All this town," she cried as the flames took her, "will come to no good of this." She was spiteful to the end, though it should be said that she had right to be.

Watching from the crowd, Emily Early of the sunny disposition smiled.

The squire himself died soon after, from a fall off his horse. And though the townfolk talked about it, they did not talk long. The squire was known to like his drink and had often taken a spill.

So the squire's son, Ewan, took over the estate, with his mother to run things as she always had. Ewan was a handsome, big boy, not overly bright. He had inherited his father's brains, though he would have done better with his mother's.

One day in this same summer Ewan saw Emily Early walking through the fields of corn, her hair yellow as flowers. In that very moment he fell in love, as if struck by lightning. And though she was not of the gentry, he determined to marry her.

His mother had misgivings about the match, but Ewan was not to be denied. By summer's end the two were wed and the widow Danforth moved into the dower house on the estate, leaving the newlyweds the fine big house.

Now, Widow Danforth kept her own counsel. She loved her son but was not blind to his faults. Neither was she charmed by his new wife. So when Ewan came to her one morning in late Autumn, she was not surprised.

"Mother, I sleep the night through," he said, "but I wake more tired than when I lie down. I fear I may be dying."

And indeed he looked it, for his handsome cheeks were now sunken and he seemed twice the age his father had been when he had had his fall.

His mother gave Ewan tea and stroked his brow and told him to bide with her a bit. She tucked him into a bed and left him to sleep the morning away, but herself she took off to the village priest.

The priest shook his head. "Call the doctor, madam," he advised. "It is no matter for me."

"And if it be witches?" asked Widow Danforth.

"The witch is dead in the cleansing fire," the priest said, and would hear no more from her, for he thought she was just a widow pushed out of her house by the new wife and come to complain.

Having got no good of the priest, Widow Danforth determined to watch the night at her son's bedfoot to see if Agnes Browne haunted him. Or if—as she really suspected—the damage was inflicted by his bride. So she sent her son back home, and waiting until he and Emily were at their dinner, sneaked up the back stairs to their bedchamber and hid herself behind the curtains, hard against the cold stone wall.

It was a long time till they came to bed. The night was dark and starless. Widow Danforth could scarcely see. But she waited patiently till all was quiet and both husband and wife slept as one.

Suddenly a candle flared to light. And Emily Early, her yellow hair spread about like a halo, rose out of the bed. She passed her hand once, twice, then a third time over the flame. She whispered something that Widow Danforth could not quite hear, then turned to her sleeping husband. Leaning over him, she blew into his mouth.

Eyes still closed, Ewan rose and stood silent by the bedfoot.

Higgety, hoggity, let me ride,
Saddle and bridle by my side,

Emily said distinctly.

At once the sleeping man got down on his hands and knees as if he were a horse, and Emily straddled him. She whipped the cord off

5

her nightdress and put it through his mouth like a bridle, and he turned into a horse. Then she jammed her heels into his sides, and they were away, the girl on the blue-eyed steed out the door, down the stairs, and lost to sight.

"Well!" said Widow Danforth, stepping out from behind the curtains. "And here's a pretty pickle. Emily has enchanted my son and ridden him off like a prize stallion—to a witches' meeting, I have no doubt of it. But what I can do to help my dear boy, I do not know." And she sat in the bedchamber the rest of the night, puzzling it over.

At last daylight came, a pink thread of light stretching from hill to vale. And back they came, rider and ridden, clattering up the stairs, through the door, and to the bedfoot, where Emily took the cord from her husband's mouth and tied up her nightdress, whispering:

> *Hoggity, higgety, let me sleep*
> *Ten miles wide, a lifetime deep.*

Then she slipped easily into the bed and drew the covers around her, while poor Ewan, back in his own shape, lay down where he was on the floor, too tired to go even one step further.

A second night the widow watched, and it was the same. But on the third, Emily Early was so full of herself that she spoke loudly. And the words she spoke over the flames were these:

> *Fire to water, water to air,*
> *Make me a horse my weight to bear.*

And when the two had galloped away into the night, Widow Danforth went to her own bed eagerly, saying, "Now I've got you, my girl."

That day Ewan visited his mother again, his blue eyes that used to be the color of dawn now the color of dusk. "I have come to make my peace with you, Mother," he said, "for I am not long for this world."

"Nonsense," said his mother, "you are but bewitched."

"Bewitched?" His puzzlement was all in the one word.

So she told him what she had seen, but he would have none of it.

"My Emily is sun and moon," he said. "You have mistook her for old Agnes Browne."

"I will prove it," said his mother. "Take no food this night. No drink, either, for I believe she has set you a potion in them to make you sleep the sounder. But put you a potion in her meat and wine, and I will show you what she does."

So that very night Ewan pretended to eat and drink, but he put a sleep draught in his wife's food. And when it came time for bed, he laid himself down as if to sleep and was quickly snoring. His young wife lay down by his side.

No sooner was the girl asleep than Widow Danforth crept from behind the curtain. She lit the candle and three times passed her hand over the flame, saying:

> *Fire to water, water to air,*
> *Make me a horse my weight to bear.*

Then she turned and leaned over the bedside and blew into Emily Early's mouth.

All this Ewan watched from the bed, without a word.

Emily stood and went to the bedfoot, where she waited, eyes closed, as patient as any mare, on her hands and knees.

"Get up, my son," Widow Danforth said, "and take the cord from her nightdress. Then place it in her mouth as if it were a bridle."

Ewan did as she bade, but most reluctantly, for he feared to hurt his pretty wife.

"Now get astride," said his mother, "and give her a kick."

"I cannot," Ewan said.

"You must," remanded his mother. "For you must ride off and see where she goes. Only be sure to return by first light."

So he gave the yellow-haired mare a kick, just a tap, and they were away, out the door, down the stairs, and out of sight.

When they returned at dawn, Widow Danforth was waiting.

"Oh, Mother," Ewan said, "I was wrong to doubt you. She is a witch as ever there was one." He climbed off Emily's back. "We galloped up one side of Bald Mountain and down the other. And there was a meeting of witches, all sitting atop their steeds. And when they saw me they cried out, 'Where is Emily, who is always so early?' And I answered, 'She is off to another meeting and sent me in her place.' That seemed to satisfy them, for they did not ask again."

"Well done, my son," the widow said. "You have more than your father's brains after all."

Ewan took the bridle out of his wife's mouth. "But what shall we do about her?" he asked.

"Why, nothing," his mother said. "There is nothing we can do."

"But she is a witch and must be punished."

"There has been punishment enough in this town already," his mother answered. "And she will serve better as a mare than ever she did as a wife. Besides, in all the excitement of the night, I have forgotten the words to change her back."

It was the one lie Widow Danforth ever spoke, but she never repented of it, especially in the years that followed, when Ewan married again and she had seven grandchildren to teach to ride the yellow-haired mare in her son's fine stable.

9

In the early 1600s Ben Jonson and William Shakespeare both wrote plays featuring witches. I was rereading the witch scene in Jonson's Masque of Queenes, which begins "Dame, dame, the watch is set: Quickly come, we all are met. From the lakes, and from the fennes, From the rockes, and from the dennes . . ." when I got the idea for this conversation, a poem for voices. It ends with a line from Shakespeare's witch scene in Macbeth. As some writer once said: "Bad poets borrow. Good ones steal."

A Conversation among Witches

WITCH 1: Here come I, from lake and fen,
             From ferny dell and rocky den.

WITCH 2: Here come I, the wind is fair.
             It carried me from my dark lair.

WITCH 3: Here come I upon my broom.
             Where can I land? Make room! Make room!

WITCH 1: Well met, well met, bewitching friends.
             Came down so fast I got the bends.

WITCH 2: Never.

WITCH 1: Ever.

WITCH 3: Don't be so clever.

WITCH 2: Have you the charm?

WITCH 3: Have you the spell?

11

WITCHES 2 AND 3: Have you the stuff to mix them well?

WITCH 1: I have it all. Have you the will?

WITCHES 2 AND 3: We have. We have. We have.

WITCH 1: Be still.

NARRATOR: They look around. They are alone.
They take out wool and wand and bone.
They take out tooth and tongue and nail.
They set the cauldron, hold the flail.

ALL THREE: By wind, by bog, by owl, by toad,
By we three bound upon this road,
By fire, water, earth, and dung,
By hemlock, hensbane, adder's tongue,
By all that's dark and all that's shade,
By all unholy, this spell's made.

Peace—the charm's wound up.

A friend of mine, Susan Schwartz, was putting together an anthology of new stories about witches called Hecate's Cauldron. (Hecate was the Greek goddess associated with the underworld, night, and witches.) She asked me to contribute. And so I wrote "Boris Chernevsky's Hands," a science fiction/fantasy story that includes the famous Russian witch, Baba Yaga.

According to the old stories, Baba Yaga rode around the forest in a mortar and pestle. Her hut strolled about on chicken feet. She was a nasty piece of business—unless she took a liking to you, which didn't happen often. I had been fascinated by stories of Baba Yaga since I was a young girl, reading about her in such books as Andrew Lang's "color" fairy books. Here, at last, was a chance for me to write my own Baba Yaga tale.

Boris Chernevsky's Hands

Boris Chernevsky, son of the Famous Flying Chernevskys and nephew to the galaxy's second-greatest juggler, woke up unevenly. That is to say, his left foot and right hand lagged behind in the morning rituals.

Feet over the side of the bed, wiggling the recalcitrant left toes and moving the sluggish right shoulder, Boris thought about his previous night's performance.

"Inept" had been Uncle Misha's kindest criticism. In fact, most of what he had yelled was untranslatable and Boris was glad that his own Russian was as fumbling as his fingers. It had not been a happy evening. He ran his slow hands through his thick blond hair and sighed, wondering—and not for the first time—if he had been adopted as an infant or exchanged *in utero* for a scholar's clone. How else to explain his general awkwardness?

He stood slowly, balancing gingerly because his left foot was now asleep, and practiced a few passes with imaginary *na* clubs. He had made his way to eight in the air and was starting an over-the-shoulder pass when the clubs slipped and clattered to the floor. Even in his imagination he was a klutz.

His Uncle Misha said it was eye and ear coordination, that the sound of the clubs and the rhythm of their passing were what made a fine juggler. And his father said the same about flying: that one had to hear the trapeze and calculate its swing by both eye and ear. But Boris was not convinced.

"It's in the hands," he said disgustedly, looking down at his five-fingered disasters. They were big-knuckled and grained like wood. He flexed them and could feel the right moving just a fraction slower than the left. "It's all in the hands. What I wouldn't give for a better pair."

"And what *would* you give, Boris Chernevsky?" The accent was Russian, or rather, Georgian. Boris looked up, expecting to see his uncle.

There was no one in the trailer.

Boris turned around twice and looked under his bed. Sometimes the circus little people played tricks, hiding in closets and making sounds like old clothes, singing. Their minds moved in strange ways, and Boris was one of their favorite gulls. He was so easily fooled.

"Would you, for example, give your soul?" The voice was less Georgian, more Siberian now. A touch of Tartar, but low and musical.

"What's a soul?" Boris asked, thinking that adopted children or clones probably weren't allowed any anyway.

"Two centuries ago," the voice said, and sighed with what sounded like a Muscovite gurgle, "everyone had a soul and no one wanted to sell. Today everyone is willing to sell, only no one seems to have one."

By this time, Boris had walked completely around the inside of the trailer, examining the undersides of chairs, lifting the samovar lid. He was convinced he was beginning to go crazy. "From dropping so many imaginary *na* clubs on my head," he told himself out loud. He sat down on one of the chairs and breathed heavily, his chin resting on his left hand. He didn't yet completely trust his right. After all, he had only been awake and moving for ten minutes.

Something materialized across the table from him. It was a tall, gaunt old woman whose hair looked as if birds might be nesting in it. Nasty birds. With razored talons and beaks permanently stained with blood. He thought he spotted guano in her bushy eyebrows.

"So," the apparition said to him, "*hands* are the topic of our discussion." Her voice, now that she was visible, was no longer melodic but grating, on the edge of a scold.

"Aren't you a bit old for such tricks, Baba?" asked Boris, trying to be both polite and steady at once. His grandmother, may she rest in pieces on the meteorite that had broken up her circus flight to a rim world, had taught him to address old women with respect. "After all, a grandmother should be . . ."

"Home tending the fire and the children, I suppose." The old woman spat into the corner, raising dust devils. "The centuries roll on and on but the Russian remains the same. The Soviets did wonders to free women up, as long as they were young. Old women, we still have the fire and the grandchildren." Her voice began to get louder and higher. *Peh*, she spat again. "Well, I for one have solved the grandchildren problem."

Boris hastened to reach out and soothe her. All he needed now, on top of last evening's disastrous performance, was to have a screaming battle with some crazy old lady when his Uncle Misha and his parents, the Famous Flying, were asleep in the small rooms on either side of the trailer. "Shh, shhh," he cautioned.

She grabbed at his reaching right hand and held it in an incredibly strong grip. Vised between her two claws, his hand could not move at all. "This, then," she asked rhetorically, "is the offending member?"

15

He pulled back with all his strength, embarrassment lending him muscles, and managed to snag the hand back. He held it under the table and tried to knead feeling back into the fingers. When he looked up at her, she was smiling at him. It was not a pretty smile.

"Yes," he admitted.

She scraped at a wen on her chin with a long, dirty fingernail. "It *seems* an ordinary enough hand," she said. "Large knuckles. Strong veins. I've known peasants and czars that would have envied you that hand."

"*Ordinary*," Boris began in a hoarse whisper, and stopped. Then, forcing himself to speak, he began again. "Ordinary is the trouble. A juggler has to have *extraordinary* hands. A juggler's hands must be spiderweb strong, bird's-wing quick." He smiled at his metaphors. Perhaps he was a poet clone.

The old woman leaned back in her chair and stared at a spot somewhere over Boris's head. Her watery blue eyes never wavered. She mumbled something under her breath, then sat forward again. "Come," she said. "I have a closetful. All you have to do is choose."

"Choose what?" asked Boris.

"*Hands!*" screeched the old woman. "Hands, you idiot. Isn't that what you want?"

"*Boris*," came his uncle's familiar voice through the thin walls. "*Boris*, I need my sleep."

"I'll come. I'll come," whispered Boris, just to get rid of the hag. He shooed her out the door with a movement of his hands. As usual, the right was a beat behind the left, even after half a morning.

He hadn't actually meant to go anywhere with her, just maneuver her out of the trailer, but when she leaped down the steps with surprising speed and climbed into a vehicle that looked like a mug with a large china steering rudder sticking out of the middle, his feet stepped forward of their own accord.

He fell down the stairs.

"Perhaps you could use a new pair of feet, too," said the old woman.

Boris stood up and automatically brushed off his clothes, a gesture his hands knew without prompting.

The old woman touched the rudder and the mug moved closer to Boris.

He looked on both sides and under the mug for evidence of its motor. It moved away from him as soundlessly as a hovercraft, but when he stuck his foot under it cautiously, he could feel no telltale movement of the air.

"How do you *do* that?" he asked.

"Do what?"

"The mug," he said.

"Magic." She made a strange gesture with her hands. "After all, I am Baba Yaga."

The name did not seem to impress Boris, who was now on his hands and knees, peering under the vehicle.

"Baba *Yaga*," the old woman repeated, as if the name itself were a charm.

"How do you do," Boris murmured, more to the ground than to her.

"You know . . . the witch . . . Russia . . . magic . . ." Her voice trailed off. When Boris made no response, she made another motion with her hands, but this time it was an Italian gesture, and not at all nice.

Boris saw the gesture and stood up. After all, the circus was his life. He knew that magic was not real, only a matter of quick hands. "Sure," he said, imitating her last gesture. His right hand clipped his left bicep. He winced.

"*Get in!*" the old woman shouted.

Boris shrugged. But his politeness was complicated by curiosity.

17

He wanted to see the inside anyway. There had to be an engine somewhere. He hoped she would let him look at it. He was good with circuitry and microchips. In a free world, he could have chosen his occupation. Perhaps he might even have been a computer programmer. But as he was a member of the Famous Flying Chernevsky family, he had no choice. He climbed over the lip of the mug and, to his chagrin, got stuck. The old woman had to pull him the rest of the way.

"You really are a klutz," she said. "Are you sure all you want is hands?"

But Boris was not listening. He was searching the inside of the giant mug.

He had just made his third trip around when it took off into the air. In less than a minute, the circus and its ring of bright trailers were only a squiggle on the horizon.

They passed quickly over the metroplexes that jigsawed across the continent, and they hovered over one of the twenty forest preserves. Baba Yaga pulled on the china rudder, and the mug dropped straight down. Boris fell sideways and clung desperately to the mug's rim. Only a foot above the treetops the mug slowed, wove its way through a complicated pattern of branches, and finally landed in a small clearing.

The old woman hopped nimbly from the flier. Boris followed more slowly.

A large presence loomed to one side of the forest clearing. It seemed to be moving toward them. An enormous bird, Boris thought. He had the impression of talons. Then he looked again. It was not a bird, but a hut, and it was walking.

Boris pointed at it. "Magic?" he asked, his mouth barely shaping the syllables.

"Feet," she answered.

"Feet?" He looked down at his feet, properly encased in Naugahyde. He looked at hers, in pointed lizard leather. Then he looked

again at the house. It was lumbering toward him on two scaly legs that ended in claws. They looked like giant replicas of the chicken feet that always floated nails-up in his mother's chicken soup. When she wasn't practicing being a Famous Flying, she made her great-great-grandmother's recipes. He preferred her in the air. "Feet," Boris said again, this time feeling slightly sick.

"But the subject is hands," Baba Yaga said. Then she turned from him and strolled over to the hut. They met halfway across the clearing. She greeted it and it gave a half bob as if curtsying, then squatted down. The old woman opened the door and went in.

Boris followed. One part of him was impressed with the special effects, the slow part of him. The fast part was already convinced it was magic.

The house inside was even more unusual than the house outside. It was one big cupboard. Doors and shelves lined every inch of wall space. And each door and cupboard carried a hand-lettered sign. The calligraphics differed from door to door, drawer to drawer, and it took a few minutes before Boris could make out the pattern. But he recognized the lettering from the days when he had helped his Uncle Boris script broadsides for their act. There was irony in the fact that he had always had a good calligraphic hand.

In Roman Bold were "Newts, eye of," "Adder, tongue of," and similar biological ingredients. Then there were botanical drawers in Carolingian Italic: "Thornapple juice," "Amanita," and the like. Along one wall, however, labeled in basic Foundational Bold, were five large cupboards marked simply: "Heads," "Hands," "Feet," "Ears," "Eyes."

The old woman walked up to that wall and threw open the door marked "Hands."

"There," she said.

Inside, on small wooden stands, were hundreds of pairs of hands.

When the light fell on them, they waved dead-white fingers as supple and mindless as worms.

"Which pair do you want to try?" Baba Yaga asked.

Boris stared. "But . . ." he managed at last, "they're miniatures."

"One size fits all," Baba Yaga said. "That's something I learned in the twentieth century." She dragged a pair out of the closet on the tiny stand. Plucking the hands from the stand, she held them in her palm. The hands began to stretch and grow, inching their way to normal size. They remained the color of custard scum.

Boris read the script on the stand to himself. "Lover's hands." He hesitated.

"Try them," the old woman said again, thrusting them at him. Her voice was compelling.

Boris took the left hand between his thumb and forefinger. The hand was as slippery as rubber and as wrinkled as a prune. He pulled it on his left hand, repelled at the feel. Slowly the hand molded itself to his, rearranging its skin over his bones. As Boris watched, the left hand took on the color of new cream, then quickly tanned to a fine, overall, healthy-looking beige. He flexed the fingers and the left hand reached over and stroked his right. At the touch, he felt a stirring of desire that seemed to move sluggishly up his arm, across his shoulder, down his back, and to grip his loins. Then the left hand reached over and picked up its mate. Without waiting for a signal from him, it lovingly pulled the right hand on, fitting each finger with infinite care.

As soon as both hands were the same tanned tone, the strong, tapered polished nails with the quarter moons winking up at him, Boris looked over at the witch.

He was surprised to see that she was no longer old but, in fact, only slightly mature, with fine bones under a translucent skin. Her blue eyes seemed to appraise him, then offer an invitation. She smiled, her mouth

21

thinned down with desire. His hands preceded him to her side, and then she was in his arms. The hands stroked her wind-tossed hair.

"You have," she breathed into his ear, "a lover's hands."

Hands! He suddenly remembered, and with his teeth he ripped the right hand off. Underneath were his own remembered big knuckles. He flexed them experimentally. They were wonderfully slow in responding.

The old woman cackled and repeated, "A lover's hands."

His slow right hand fought with the left but managed at last to scratch off the outer layer. His left hand felt raw, dry, but comfortingly familiar.

The old woman was still smiling an invitation. She had crooked teeth and large pores. There was a dark moustache on her upper lip.

Boris picked up the discarded hands by the tips of the fingers and held them up before the witch's watery blue eyes. "Not *these* hands," he said.

She was already reaching into the closet for another pair.

Boris pulled the hands on quickly, glancing only briefly at the label. "Surgeon's hands." They were supple-fingered and moved nervously in the air, as if searching for something to do. Finally they hovered over Baba Yaga's forehead. Boris felt as if he had eyes in his fingertips, and suddenly he saw the old woman's skin as a map stretched across a landscape of muscle and bone. He could sense the subtle traceries of veins and read the directions of the bloodlines. His right hand moved down the bridge of her nose, turned left at the cheek, and descended to her chin. The second finger tapped her wen, and he could hear the faint echo of his knock.

"I could remove that easily," he found himself saying.

The witch pulled the surgeon's hands from him herself. "Leave me my wen. Leave me my own face," she said angrily. "It is the stage setting for my magic. Surgeon's hands indeed."

Remembering the clowns in their makeup, the wire-walkers in their sequined leotards, the ringmaster in his tie and tails, costumes that had not changed over the centuries of circus, Boris had to agree. He looked down again at his own hands. He moved the fingers. The rights were still laggards. But for the first time he heard and saw how they moved. He dropped his hands to his sides and beat a tattoo on his outer thighs. Three against two went the rhythm, the left hitting the faster beat. He increased it to seven against five and smiled. The right would always be slower, he knew that now.

"It's not in the hands," he said.

Baba Yaga looked at him quizzically. Running a hand through her bird's-nest hair and fluffing up her eyebrows, she spoke. But it was Uncle Boris's voice that emerged between her crooked teeth: "Hands are the daughters of the eye and ear."

"How do you *do* that?" Boris asked.

"Magic," she answered, smiling. She moved her fingers mysteriously, then turned and closed the cupboard doors.

Boris smiled at her back and moved his own fingers in imitation. Then he went out the door of the house and fell down the steps.

"Maybe you'd like a new pair of feet," the witch called after him. "I have Fred Astaire's. I have John Travolta's. I have Michael Jackson's. I have Muhammad Ali's." She came out of the house, caught up with Boris, and pulled him to a standing position.

"Were they jugglers?" asked Boris.

"No," Baba Yaga said, shaking her head. "No. But they had soul."

Boris didn't answer. Instead he climbed into the mug and gazed fondly at his hands as the mug took off and headed toward the horizon and home.

Why a cat? In folklore, witches have familiar spirits or, more commonly, familiars, who do their bidding. The animal usually regarded as a witch's familiar is the cat, though there is occasional mention of an owl or a toad.

I am a cat person myself. My husband prefers dogs. Over the years we have had an English setter (Arwen Evenstar), a springer spaniel (Aragorn Strider), and lots of cats. There were Nuncle, Math, and Penny Dreadful when we lived in New York City, and once we moved to the country, many more: Colin, Dickon, Noodge, Amber, and the family favorite, a orange tom with double paws, Pod.

Witch's Cat

I am a companion
both dark and light,
I am a shadow
on the edge of sight,
I am a whisper
in the morning grass,
I am a motion
in the tinted glass,
I am a howl
when night is done,
I am a dust mote
in the morning sun,
I am a stroking
beneath your hand,
I am a message
at your command.

My friend Christine Crow and I were walking into town and she was wearing
a Medusa necklace so, of course, we talked about the story of the hero Perseus.
It was she who mentioned the phrase "the passing of the eye," which gave me
this entire short-short story in an instant. It was two weeks later, after a trip to
the Highlands of Scotland, that I finally got around to writing it down.
Usually stories come to me in bits and pieces. Only a rare one comes whole.

The Passing of the Eye

The hero paused outside the cave, listening to an odd sound that echoed from within. It was a loud, high cackling. He could scarcely make it out.

> *Pass the eye, pass the eye;*
> *One, two, let it by.*

It didn't make any sense, but then he was on a quest and sense was hardly ever part of that.

He smiled his hero smile, drew his hero sword—the one with the witch-bane silver handle—and went in.

The cave was very smoky and he knew smoke was bad for his health. He wondered if there was a section of the cave reserved for nonsmokers. A dark, peaty aroma rose up from the fire. Peering through the haze, he was finally able to make out the figures of three alien creatures hunched over a pot, passing something around.

He knew just what to do. It was in all the quest brochures. Stepping forward, he grabbed the token they were passing with his left hand, the one without the sword.

25

"You must give me what I want," he said. "And then I shall return this to you." The brochures all said that a true hero was decisive and stuck by his decisions, right or wrong. But then he noticed that the aliens weren't alien at all, but were women.

"I beg your pardon, gentle persons," he said, for it was a time of special courtesy and favors toward women.

"That for your pardon!" shouted one of the women. "Give it back."

Then the hero noticed they were *old* women. One of them even had a smattering of white whiskers on her chin. "I truly beg your pardon, gentle persons of great life span." For it was also a time of special courtesy and favors toward the elderly.

"Back *now!*" said the second old woman, waving her arms about.

It was then that he noticed that the three of them were unsighted. He was appalled at his own lack of awareness. "I beg your pardon indeed, visually challenged gentle persons of great life span."

"Give us back the eye!" the third one bellowed.

Only then did he see that the token in his hand was, truly, an eye. It winked up at him with an especially knowing look, as if heroes were as common as dirt in that cave. He handed the eye back at once.

The first old woman grabbed it. "I'll give you visually challenged, you hiccup!" she said. "Without that eye we're blind as bats." She shared the eye around with her sisters, who each stared at the hero in turn.

Then they chopped him up for kindling. And he never got to finish his journey, killing princesses, marrying dragons, or whatever politically correct thing is done on quests these days.

Just as well.

Stories start in two places, one outside the writer, one inside. I had begun this story because I loved the old fairy tales that open with a king and queen who want a child, tales like "Snow White." But my story only went as far as the queen visiting the three witch sisters. I did not know where to go from that traditional opening. And so the story starter sat in my file drawer for several years. Occasionally I would take it out and read it aloud, hoping that inspiration would strike.

Then one day, in the shower (where inspiration often strikes, wetly and awkwardly), I knew what the story was about. Inspiration had come from inside. I was thinking about my mother, dead some twelve years. And thinking about my teenage daughter, struggling with the fact that her mother was a well-known writer. This is a story about daughters carrying their mothers' images through their lives, something they feel (even if unconsciously) they have to live up to. And knowing that, I was able to finish the story.

This is the third piece where the number three crops up; it is a magical number, whether there are three little pigs, three blind mice, or three witch sisters.

The Face in the Cloth

There were once a King and Queen so in love with one another that they could not bear to be parted, even for a day. To seal their bond, they desperately wanted a child. The King had even made a cradle of oak for the babe with his own hands and placed it by their great canopied bed. But year in and year out, the cradle stood empty.

At last, one night when the King was fast asleep, the Queen left their bed. She cast one long, lingering glance at her husband, then, disguising herself with a shawl around her head, she crept out of the castle, for the first time alone. She was bound for a nearby forest where

27

she had heard that three witch sisters lived. The Queen had been told that they might give her what she most desired by taking from her what she least desired to give.

But I have so much, she thought as she ran through the woods. *Gold and jewels beyond counting. Even the diamond that the King himself put on my hand and from which I would hate to be parted. But though it is probably what I would least desire to give, I would give it gladly in order to have a child.*

The witches' hut squatted in the middle of the wood, and through its window the Queen saw the three old sisters sitting by the fire, chanting a spell as soft as a cradle song:

> *Needle and scissors,*
> *Scissors and pins,*
> *Where one life ends,*
> *Another begins.*

And suiting their actions to the words, the three snipped and sewed, snipped and sewed with an invisible thread over and over and over again.

The night was so dark and the three slouching sisters so strange that the Queen was quite terrified. But her need was even greater than her fear. She scratched upon the window, and the three looked up from their work.

"Come in," they called out in a single voice.

So she had to go, pulled into the hut by that invisible thread.

"What do you want, my dear?" said the first old sister to the Queen, through the pins she held in her mouth.

"I want a child," said the Queen.

"When do you want it?" asked the second sister, who held a needle high above her head.

"As soon as I can get it," said the Queen, more boldly now.

"And what will you give for it?" asked the third, snipping her scissors ominously.

"Whatever is needed," replied the Queen. Nervously she turned the ring with the diamond around her finger.

The three witches smiled at one another. Then they each held up a hand with the thumb and forefinger touching in a circle.

"Go," they said. "It is done. All we ask is to be at the birthing to sew the swaddling clothes."

The Queen stood still as stone, a river of feeling washing around her. She had been prepared to gift them a fortune. What they asked was so simple, she agreed at once. Then she turned and ran out of the hut all the way to the castle. She never looked back.

Less than a year later, the Queen was brought to childbed. In her great joy at having a child, she had forgotten to mention her promise to the King. And then in great pain in her labor—and because it had been such a small promise after all—she forgot to tell him altogether.

As the Queen lay in her canopied bed, there came a knock on the castle door. When the guards opened it, who should be standing there but three slouching old women.

"We have come to be with the Queen," said the one with pins in her mouth.

The guards shook their heads.

"The Queen promised we could make the swaddling cloth," said the second, holding her needle high over her head.

"We must be by her side," said the third, snapping her scissors.

One guard was sent to tell the King.

The King came to the castle door, his face red with anger, his brow wreathed with sweat.

"The Queen told me of no such promise," he said. "And she tells me everything. What possesses you to bother a man at a time like this? Begone." He dismissed them with a wave of his hand.

But before the guards could shut the door upon the ancient sisters, the one with the scissors called out, "Beware, O King, of promises given." Then all three chanted:

> *Needle and scissors,*
> *Scissors and pins,*
> *Where one life ends,*
> *Another begins.*

The second old woman put her hands above her head and made a circle with her forefinger and thumb. But the one with the pins in her mouth thrust a piece of cloth into the King's hand.

"It is for the babe," she said. "Because of the Queen's desire."

Then the three left the castle and were not seen there again.

The King started to look down at the cloth, but there came a loud cry from the bedchamber. He ran back along the corridors, and when he entered the bedroom door, the doctor turned around, a newborn child, still red with birth blood, in his hands.

"It is a girl, Sire," he said.

There was a murmur of praise from the attending women.

The King put out his hands to receive the child and, for the first time, really noticed the cloth he was holding. It was pure white, edged with lace. As he looked at it, his wife's likeness began to appear on it slowly, as if being stitched in with a crimson thread. First the eyes he so loved; then the elegant nose; the soft, full mouth; the dimpled chin.

The King was about to remark on it when the midwife cried out, "The Queen, Sire. She is dead." And at the same moment, the doctor put the child into his hands.

The royal funeral and the royal christening were held on the same day, and no one in the kingdom knew whether to laugh or cry except the babe, who did both.

Since the King could not bear to part with his wife entirely, he had the cloth with her likeness sewed into the baby's cloak so that, wherever she went, the Princess carried her mother's face.

As she outgrew one cloak, the white lace was cut away from the old and sewn into the new. And in this way the Princess was never without the panel bearing her mother's portrait; nor was she ever allowed to wander far from her father's watchful eyes. Her life was measured by the size of the cloaks, which were cut bigger each year, and by the likeness of her mother, which seemed to get bigger as well.

The Princess grew taller, but she did not grow stronger. She was like a pale copy of her mother. There was never a time that the bloom of health sat on her cheeks. She remained the color of skimmed milk, the color of ocean foam, the color of second-day snow. She was always cold, sitting huddled for warmth inside her picture cloak even on the hottest days, and nothing could part her from it.

The King despaired of his daughter's health, but neither the royal physicians nor philosophers could help. He turned to necromancers and stargazers, to herbalists and diviners. They pushed and prodded and prayed over the Princess. They examined the soles of her feet and the movement of her stars. But still she sat cold and whey-colored, wrapped in her cloak.

At last one night, when everyone was fast asleep, the King left his bed and crept out of the castle alone. He had heard that there were three witch sisters who lived nearby who might give him what he most desired by taking from him what he least desired to give. Having lost his Queen, he knew there was nothing else he would hate losing—not his fortune, his kingdom, or his throne. He would give it all up gladly to see his daughter, who was his wife's pale reflection, sing and dance and run.

The witches' hut squatted in the middle of the wood, and through its window the King saw the three old sisters. He did not recognize them, but they knew him at once.

"Come in, come in," they called out, though he had not knocked. And he was drawn into the hut as if pulled by an invisible thread.

"We know what you want," said the first.

"We can give you what you desire," said the second.

"By taking what you least wish to give," said the third.

"I have already lost my Queen," he said. "So anything else I have is yours, so long as my daughter is granted a measure of health." And he started to twist off the ring he wore on his third finger, the ring his wife had been pledged with, to give to the three sisters to seal his part of the bargain.

"Then you must give us—your daughter," said the three.

The King was stunned. For a moment the only sound in the hut was the crackle of fire in the hearth.

"*Never!*" he thundered at last. "What you ask is impossible."

"What *you* ask is impossible," said the first old woman. "Nonetheless, we promise it will be so." She stood. "But if your daughter does not come to us, her life will be worth no more than this." She took a pin from her mouth and held it up. It caught the firelight for a moment. Only a moment.

The King stared. "I know you," he said slowly. "I have seen you before."

The second sister nodded. "Our lives have been sewn together by a queen's desire," she said. She pulled the needle through a piece of cloth she was holding and drew the thread through in a slow, measured stitch.

33

The third sister began to chant, and at each beat her scissors snapped together:

Needle and scissors,
Scissors and pins,
Where one life ends,
Another begins.

The King cursed them thoroughly, his words hoarse as a rote of war, and left. But partway through the forest, he thought of his daughter asleep like a waning moon, and wept.

For days he raged in the palace, and his courtiers felt his tongue as painfully as if it were a whip. Even his daughter, usually silent in her shroudlike cloak, cried out.

"Father," she said, "your anger unravels the kingdom, pulling at its loosest threads. What is it? What can I do?" As she spoke, she clutched the cloak more firmly about her shoulders, and the King could swear that the portrait of his wife moved, the lips opening and closing as if the image spoke as well.

The King shook his head and put his hands to his face. "You are all I have left of her," he mumbled. "And now I must let you go."

The Princess did not understand, but she put her small faded hands on his. "You must do what you must do, my father," she said.

And though he did not quite understand the why of it, the King brought his daughter into the wood the next night after dark. Setting her on his horse and holding the bridle himself, he led her along the path to the hut of the three crones.

At the door he kissed her once on each cheek and then tenderly kissed the image on her cloak. Then, mounting his horse, he galloped away without once looking back.

Behind him the briars closed over the path, and the forest was still.

Once her father had left, the Princess looked around the dark clearing. When no one came to fetch her, she knocked upon the door of the little hut. Getting no answer, she pushed the door open and went in.

The hut was empty, though a fire burned merrily in the hearth. The table was set, and beside the wooden plate were three objects: a needle, a pair of scissors, and a pin. On the hearth wall, engraved in the stone, was a poem. The Princess went over to the fire to read it:

Needle and scissors,
Scissors and pins,
Where one life ends,
Another begins.

How strange, thought the Princess, shivering inside her cloak. She looked around the little hut, found a bed with a wooden headboard shaped like a loom, lay down upon the bed, and pulling the cloak around her even more tightly, slept.

In the morning, when the Princess woke, she was still alone, but there was food on the table, steaming hot. She rose and made a feeble toilette, for there were no mirrors on the walls, and ate the food. All the while she toyed with the needle, scissors, and pin by her plate. She longed for her father and the familiarity of the court, but her father had left her at the hut, and being an obedient child, she stayed.

As she finished her meal, the hearthfire went out, and soon the hut grew chilly. So the Princess went outside and sat on a wooden bench by the door. Sunlight illuminated the clearing and wrapped around

35

her shoulders like a golden cloak. Alternately she dozed and woke and dozed again until it grew dark.

When she went inside the hut, the table was once more set with food, and this time she ate eagerly, then went to sleep, dreaming of the needle and scissors and pin. In her dream they danced away from her, refusing to bow when she bade them.

She woke to a cold dawn. The meal was ready, and the smell of it, threading through the hut, got her up. She wondered briefly what hands had done all the work, but, being a princess and used to being served, she did not wonder about it very long.

When she went outside to sit in the sun, she sang snatches of old songs to keep herself company. The sound of her own voice, tentative and slightly off key, was like an old friend. The tune kept running around and around in her head, and though she did not know where she had heard it before, it fitted perfectly the words carved over the hearth:

> *Needle and scissors,*
> *Scissors and pins,*
> *Where one life ends,*
> *Another begins.*

"This is certainly true," she told herself, "for my life here in the forest is different from my life in the castle, though I myself do not feel changed." And she shivered and pulled the cloak around her.

Several times she stood and walked about the clearing, looking for the path that led out. But it was gone. The brambles were laced firmly together like stitches on a quilt, and when she put a hand to them, a thorn pierced her palm and the blood dripped down onto her cloak, spotting the portrait of her mother and making it look as if she were crying red tears.

It was then the Princess knew that she had been abandoned to the magic in the forest. She wondered that she was not more afraid, and tried out different emotions: first fear, then bewilderment, then loneliness; but none of them seemed quite real to her. What she felt, she decided at last, was a kind of lightness, a giddiness, as if she had lost her center, as if she were a balloon, untethered and ready—at last—to let go.

"What a goose I have become," she said aloud. "One or two days without the prattle of courtiers, and I am talking to myself."

But her own voice was a comfort, and she smiled. Then, settling her cloak more firmly about her shoulders, she went back to the hut.

She counted the meager furnishings of the hut as if she were telling beads on a string: door, window, hearth, table, chair, bed. *I wish there were something to* do, she thought to herself. And as she turned around, the needle on the table was glowing as if a bit of fire had caught in its eye.

She went over to the table and picked up the needle, scissors, and pin and carried them to the hearth. Spreading her cloak on the stones, though careful to keep her mother's image facing up, she sat.

If I just had some thread, she thought.

Just then she noticed the panel with her mother's portrait. For the first time it seemed small and crowded, spotted from the years. The curls were old-fashioned and overwrought, the mouth a little slack, the chin a touch weak.

"Perhaps if I could borrow a bit of thread from this embroidery," she whispered, "just a bit where it will not be noticed. As I am alone, no one will know but me."

Slowly she began to pick out the crimson thread along one of the tiny curls. She heard a deep sigh as she started, as if it came from the cloak, then realized it had been her own breath that had made the sound. She wound up the thread around the pin until she had quite

37

a lot of it. Then she snipped off the end, knotted it, threaded the needle—and stopped.

What am I to sew upon? she wondered. All she had was what she wore. Still, as she had a great need to keep herself busy and nothing else to do, she decided to embroider designs along the edges of her cloak. So she began with what she knew. On the grey panels she sewed a picture of her own castle. It was so real, it seemed as if its banners fluttered in a westerly wind. And as it grew, turret by turret, she began to feel a little warmer, a little more at home.

She worked until it was time to eat, but as she had been in the hut all the while, no magical servants had set the table. So she hunted around the cupboards herself until she found bread and cheese and a pitcher of milk. After making herself a scanty meal, she cleaned away the dishes, then lay down on the bed and was soon asleep.

In the morning she was up with the dawn. She cut herself some bread, poured some milk, and took the meal outside, where she continued to sew. She gave the castle lancet windows, a Lady chapel, cows grazing in the outlying fields, and a moat in which golden carp swam about, their fins stroking the water and making little waves that moved beneath her hand.

When the first bit of thread was used up, she picked out another section of the portrait, all of the curls and a part of the chin. With that thread she embroidered a forest around the castle, where brachet hounds, noses to the ground, sought a scent; a deer started; and a fox lay hidden in a rambling thicket, its ears twitching as the dogs coursed by. She could almost remark their baying, now near, now far away. Then, in the middle of the forest—with a third piece of thread—the Princess sewed the hut. Beneath the hut, as she sewed, letters appeared, though she did not touch them.

Needle and scissors,
Scissors and pins,
Where one life ends,
Another begins.

She said the words aloud, and as she spoke, puffs of smoke appeared above the embroidered chimney in the hut. It reminded her that it was time to eat.

Stretching, she stood and went into the little house. The bread was gone. She searched the cupboards and could find no more, but there was flour and salt, and so she made herself some flat cakes that she baked in an oven set into the stone of the fireplace. She knew that the smoke from her baking was sending soft clouds above the hut.

While the bread baked and the sweet smell embroidered the air, the Princess went back outside. She unraveled more threads from her mother's image: the nose, the mouth, the startled eyes. And with that thread she traced a winding path from the crimson castle with the fluttering banners to the crimson hut with the crown of smoke.

As she sewed, it seemed to her that she could hear the sound of birds—the rapid flutings of a thrush and the *jug-jug-jug* of a nightingale—and that they came not from the real forest around her but from the cloak. Then she heard, from the very heart of her lap work, the deep, brassy voice of a hunting horn summoning her home.

Looking up from her work, she saw that the brambles around the hut were beginning to part and there was a path heading north toward the castle.

She jumped up, tumbling needle and scissors, pin and cloak to the ground, and took a step toward the beckoning path. Then she stopped. The smell of fresh bread stayed her. The embroidery was not yet done. She knew that she had to sew her own portrait: a girl with

39

crimson cheeks and hair tumbled to her shoulders, walking the path alone. She had to use up the rest of her mother's thread before she was free.

Turning back toward the hut, she saw three old women standing in the doorway, their faces familiar. They smiled and nodded to her, holding out their hands.

The first old woman had the needle and pin nestled in her palm. The second held the scissors by the blades, handles offered. The third old woman shook out the cloak, and as she did so, a breeze stirred the trees in the clearing.

The Princess smiled back at them. She held out her hands to receive their gifts. When she was done with the embroidery, though it was hard to part with it, she would give them the cloak. She knew that once it was given, she could go.

I was coming home on a train when the idea of a child in elementary school writing an assigned essay on the topic "What I Want to Be When I Grow Up" popped into my head. Except that this child would talk about following the family's traditional occupation—magic.

It was about four days before I could get to the typewriter and actually make a draft of that idea.

I have a brother-in-law who is a pharmaceuticals salesman in Phoenix, Arizona, and the drug-dealing jokes come from him.

The real Dr. Dee was a famous Elizabethan sorcerer who lived in England. I thought it would be fun to give him a whole branch of American descendants. (I am not sure he had any children at all.)

When I Grow Up,
by Michael Dee

When I grow up, I want to be a warlock. It runs in our family.

Not my dad. He's a pharmaceuticals salesman. Mom calls him a drug dealer, but he sells things like Tylenol Plus and constipation aids to doctors and medical centers. Granddad says magic skips a Dee every few generations.

But me—I've got the warlock genes. Granddad says I've got the "mickey," too. That sounds too much like Disney for me. I think he means I've got the spunk, the spark, the guts for it.

The dictionary says a warlock is a male witch or a man practicing the black arts. But Granddad has given me a list of names to memorize and I like those much better. The list is almost like a poem.

Mage.
Magus.
Magician.
Shaman.
Diviner.
Hex.

He says there are many other names, some of them not to be said in front of women or the faint-hearted. I think he means they are swears, but I am not sure.

When I get older I will wear a long black robe with a neat pointy hood. I'll be allowed to tie the robe with a special belt, just like they do in karate. Only the warlock belt is more like a rope with special medals on it, for the spells and things. Granddad's got thirteen different ones, including a cat in silver, a circle with an **X** in it in gold, and something that looks like three legs running, which is sort of weird but also sort of neat. The medals are awarded as you get better at your spells, a little like Boy Scout badges, I guess, only more important since it's your life's work.

There's an oath, too, only I am not allowed to write it down. For one, it would scorch the very paper, and for another, people who are not warlocks aren't supposed to hear it. But it's all about honesty and loyalty to the community and doing good and following the healer's art.

I will be my granddad's apprentice for seven years and then a journeyman for seven more before becoming a high mage or a master warlock. That sounds like a long time, I know, but Granddad says if I start now, when I am seventeen I will be a journeyman, and a master at twenty-four. That's about when someone learning to be a doctor would just first be getting his or her hands on a patient. And I can still

go to college at the same time. Or be a rock star, which is the *other* thing I want to be.

Now the bad things. I will have a lot to memorize, like the words of spells and the right way to summon a demon or angel. You have to get it right, or—oh, boy! I had a great-uncle who got the words reversed on one summons, my granddad said, and called a rain demon when he really wanted to summon a drain demon to fix the kitchen sink. You've heard of the Johnstown Flood? Well, that was my great-uncle Paul's doing.

And then there are the plants. Do you *know* how many plants there are? Even here in Westchester County? Not only do I have to know the names—common, technical (that means Latin!), and magical, I also have to know when they grow, where they grow, and all about the uses of root, leaf, bud, flower, stamen, and pistil. (I used to think Granddad meant a pistol, like a gun, and wondered which flowers had those.) In fact, I will probably have to major in botany in college just to get it all right. Dad insists that his pharmaceuticals can do everything that plants do and more. He and Granddad get into arguments about it every time Granddad comes to dinner. Mom calls it our own private drug war.

Also, I have to know the difference between the Good Arts and the Bad Arts (not black arts, as people who don't know any better call them). The problem is, the Bad Arts are really more fun to do, like turning people into newts and toilet-papering the top of a church tower. I have to know the difference, and know how to do them all. And then *NOT* do the Bad Arts. Granddad explained that in order to know what to avoid, I have to learn the bad stuff as thoroughly as the good. Mom doesn't let me practice any of it at home. She says it all smells funny, and maybe it does. When you are working with spells, though, you don't smell it yourself.

So every day after school, and after baseball practice, I spend an hour at Granddad's house practicing my spelling. And I have a lesson every Saturday morning and a test on things once a month, usually on the thirteenth, because numbers are real important, too.

That's all I can think to write about What I Want to Be When I Grow Up. I hope this is what you wanted. And I hope you believe me and don't think I am making this up, like Mrs. Cassiday did last year when she gave us the same assignment. Being a newt, even for just a few minutes, is really very uncomfortable. If you ask her directly, she will probably tell you.

—Michael Dee

No study of wizards and witches can ignore the Greek philosopher and mage Pythagoras, who lived more than two thousand five hundred years ago. I read about his exploits—including the three mentioned in this poem—in a book called Witches and Sorcerers *by Arkon Dauraul. The list of Pythagoras's exploits even contains accounts of his having been in two places simultaneously, journeying through time and space, and having a thigh made of purest gold. In other words, though he was a real person, a famous mathematician, the rest is folklore. But I could not resist writing a poem about him.*

Pythagoras

Noble wizard, all in white,
Called an eagle down from flight.
On his hand he bade it sit,
Stroked its head, and ate with it.

Noble wizard, all in white,
Calmed a bear prepared to bite.
"Brother," he said in its ear,
"Do not chew whilst I am here."

Noble wizard, all in white,
Near a stream both quick and bright,
Passed with neither brag nor fuss.
Stream cried, "Hail, Pythagoras."

This story owes something to Hans Christian Andersen's "Snow Queen," which I loved as a child. I borrowed the friendship between the boy and girl, and his name—Kay—at least. I can only guess at what else was borrowed in the fifty years I have loved that story.

I have also borrowed from myself. Long ago I wrote a poem in which the trees had "green rosaries of buds," and I used that phrase again here. Another poem had someone with hands "resting like withered leaves on his breast." When I like one of my own lines, I like it a lot!

But mostly this story is about promises. I am a great one for promises. And I keep them.

The Promise

There were once fond and loving friends who were delivered of children on the same day and hour. They rejoiced in their good fortune and named the boy Kay and the girl Kaya, promising each other that the two children would never be parted. Indeed, they spoke often of that promise to the boy and girl. And the children, a laughing, talkative pair, took up the promise as their own and gave it freely one to the other.

But the fond friends died within days of one another, when the children were thirteen years old. The promise was not kept. Kay and Kaya were sent off to a distant city to live with their relatives, the boy to stay with an old uncle who was a sorcerer and the girl to a convent whose abbess was her aunt.

When they arrived at the city and stood hand in hand by the carriage, the old uncle looked them over and frowned. He pulled thoughtfully at the greying ends of his moustache, then dismissed the

47

boy with a shrug. But the girl, Kaya, took his heart. He swore silently by the dark gods he worshiped that he would marry her when she came of age.

This decision the sorcerer did not speak at once, for he was used to a life built upon secrets that he rubbed to himself in the silence of his room till they festered like sores. Yet by the time he had delivered Kaya to the convent's care, he'd tumbled his secret into the air, for the girl's garrulous open nature had worked upon him and forced it out.

"I shall marry this girl, Mother," he said to the old abbess. "When she is sixteen I shall come for her."

Kaya shrank back from each syllable and her bright little face darkened. She began to tremble. "It is Kay I am to marry," she cried. "It was promised."

The sorcerer did not seem to hear. He spoke directly to the abbess. "Treat the girl well. I shall come for her. I swear it."

The abbess did not reply, for she was vowed to silence. But she held the trembling girl to her all the while the sorcerer was near. And when he had departed, dragging Kay after him, the abbess brought the girl into the convent and shut the gates after them with a mighty clang, as if the noise alone could drive out demons.

The nuns went their silent ways, but Kaya wept. She had not their assurances. She alone among them had not been promised heaven. She played and read and sat wrapped in her own misery by the convent pool. Under the willow, with its green rosary of buds, where only the whisper of the water and tree disturbed the convent silence, Kaya grew into a woman. She was allowed to speak but did not, except to the tree and the pool, for they alone returned her answers.

Now, though he had ignored it, the sorcerer had heard Kaya's cry. It shook his dark pride. And when he returned with Kay to their rooms, his heart was already hardened toward the boy, Kaya's promised one. Whereas he might have been a tolerant master, he was now a cruel one; whereas he might have pitied the boy's loneliness, now he felt no pity at all.

Kay bore it bravely for a long while—indeed he had no reason to do otherwise. He expected nothing from the old man and so he was not disappointed when nothing was his lot.

But at night, when the sorcerer was asleep, hands resting like withered leaves on his breast, the boy would lift the curtain of the single window in his room and look out at the glittering stars. He would lean on his elbows and breathe half-remembered prayers whose words fell away from him with every passing day. As each word slipped away from memory, he substituted the one name he could recall: Kaya.

One night, when Kay was thus occupied, the old sorcerer awoke. The sounds of the boy's prayers were small daggers in his heart, for innocent prayer is the enemy of sorcery. He lifted himself from his bed and came silently to the boy's room.

There, elbows on the windowsill, Kay stuttered at the stars:

> *And though I walk through . . .*
> *The shadowed valley . . .*
> *. . . I will not fear for . . .*
> *. . . Oh, Kaya, Kaya . . . be with me.*

"Kaya will never be with you," cried the old man, striking the boy with his hand.

As Kay cringed from the unexpected blow, the sorcerer moved his hand in a circle. "You *will* fear," he spat out. "And you will not pray. Indeed you will say not another word more." And he cast a spell on the boy.

49

Kay would have cried out then, more in anger than in fear, but he could not. His tongue cleaved to the roof of his mouth. His lips could not part. The sorcerer's magic had sealed them. He was as dumb as a beast.

"Go to bed," said the sorcerer, and turned in bleak triumph back to his own sleep.

But wordless, Kay was the enemy that, with words, he would never have been. He determined to resist the old man. Yet he was too young and too weak to fight the sorcerer outright. His resistance was a sly one. He began to undo the old man's long, tortuous spells. He dropped beakers in which potions were kept. He swept dust across the pentagram lines. He tore holes like mouse bites from the pages of the sorcerer's great books. And with each small act of resistance, Kay began to remember more words from his prayers, until at last he could recall them all and repeat them in his head, though the words could not pass his mouth.

One evening, in the dead part of winter, Kay was ripping a snippet from *The Book of Night*. He used his nails, which had grown long and sharp in the sorcerer's service. Carefully he carved out a section in imitation of a mouse bite.

Suddenly the sorcerer swooped down on him as if from a great height.

"It is *you*. It has been you all this time, breaking my spells and undoing my enchantments. Well, I will make an enchantment you cannot break," the old man screamed.

The boy did not dare look at the sorcerer straight on, yet he did not dare look away. He clouded his eyes over in order not to see the old man clearly.

"All your defiances are for nothing," said the sorcerer. "You are lost—and your Kaya is lost to you forever."

At Kaya's name, the boy leaped at the sorcerer's eyes and would have found them with his nails if the old man had not quickly spat out a spell:

Beast to fish
In virgin well,
A kiss alone
Can break the spell.

At the words, Kay felt his bones shrinking, contracting, growing smaller and lighter. His arms clung to his sides. His feet grew together. The air in his lungs was hot and seared his throat. He tried to breathe and could not. He gasped and gasped, and at each gasp the sorcerer laughed at him.

"You will leap upon no one again," the old man said. "Your only leaping shall be done in a pool." He threw Kay, who was now a silver carp, into a bucket of dirty water. Then, leaning over the bucket, where the fish swam around in maddened circles, the old man laughed again. "I shall show you your Kaya. You shall see her daily, and she you, but she will not be pleased with your appearance. A fish is the one pet the nuns are allowed. You shall be as chaste as they, and I shall have your Kaya."

The sorcerer placed the bucket by his bed, where he slept the rest of the night in dreamless sleep. In the morning he delivered the bucket to the convent with the admonition that none but Kaya should tend the fish.

The nun who took the carp in its bucket said nothing in thanks. Instead she went straight to the pool, where Kaya sat wrapped in her own silences, her fingers idling in the water. The nun tapped the girl on the shoulder and Kaya looked up, her oval face framed by a halo of black hair.

51

Without further ceremony, the nun dumped the water-smooth silver fish into the pool. It circled once and came in under Kaya's fingers.

The girl was so frightened by this, she pulled her hand from the water and stared. At that, the fish gave a bubbling sigh and dove to the bottom of the pool. It did not come up again.

Kaya stood up and went inside.

But the next morning she was by the pool again. Sadness, like an old habit, claimed her. And when she put her fingers in the pool, drawing wavery pictures in the water, the great fish surfaced and circled them. And as he swam, the sunlight was caught in his scales and made iridescent patterns on the steep pool sides.

"What a strange and beautiful fish," said Kaya, trying out her words in the convent silence. "I wish you were mine, for I have no one at all."

At that, the carp circled under the green fingers of the willow tree and back again to the girl, as if offering itself. And though she could not bear to feel its cold, scaly skin, Kaya fed the fish from her own fingers, dropping the crumbs of hard bread moments before the fish's mouth could touch her hands.

Less than a week later the old sorcerer came to the convent and ordered Kaya brought to him. He stood, gnarled and frowning, in his black coat as the girl came to the door.

"It has been determined," he said, though he did not say by whom, "that today we shall be wed."

Kaya, who had not spoken to another human being since arriving at the convent, moved away from his words. She could find only one of her own in return.

"Kay," she said.

At the name, the sorcerer smiled, showing grey teeth beneath his moustache. "Kay cannot marry you."

"But we were promised to each other! Is he dead?"

The sorcerer's magic impelled him to the truth, but a strange truth, warped to his own purpose. "Not dead. But deeply changed, child. Changed beyond recognition. He does not want you as he is."

"He does not want me?"

"No."

Kaya began to weep and her old words tumbled between them. "I do not care. I want Kay. It was promised. It must be so."

The sorcerer was angry, but he could do no magic here, at the convent door. There was no way to stop the girl's tongue save in his own house, in his own time.

"If Kay will not have me, no man will have me," said Kaya. "I shall become one of the nuns."

"You have been promised to me instead. I am to take Kay's place," said the old man, neglecting to mention that he himself was the one who had made the promise.

Kaya stopped crying. All her life she had been told about the power of promises. A promise given must be kept. She could not dismiss it lightly.

The sorcerer knew this. He saw his words working a subtle magic on Kaya's face. Seeing her consideration, he took it as acceptance. "The gift I sent, the carp. It should be nicely fatted by now. We shall have it today for our wedding feast."

Kaya looked clearly at the sorcerer for the first time. He stood before her, playing idly with the iron button of his cloak. The threat behind his gentle tone was revealed by his casual cruelty to her fish. Suddenly she knew his promise for a lie. Still, she saw no way to escape him. So, to gain a little more time to think of a solution, she gave a lie in return.

"Tomorrow," she said.

"Tomorrow," said the old man, and left with a quick step.

Kaya waited until night, well past the hour of compline, when the nuns spoke their last prayers in the candlelit chapel. Then, knowing the sisters were all asleep, Kaya rose and wrapped her cloak around her thin nightdress. She went out into the garden and stood by the abbess's pool.

"Fish," she called softly, "fish, come up."

The carp swam lazily to the surface. He never slept, but he lay for hours on the cool bottom of the pool. Although he was sleepless, he was not without dreams.

"*He* would marry me," said Kaya in a whisper. "*He* would serve you for the wedding feast." And though she did not name the sorcerer in that holy place, the fish knew and shuddered.

"Do not fear, little friend," said the girl. "He shall have neither of us. I will drown you in the air and myself in the pool. This I promise. And we shall be together in paradise."

She took off her cloak and laid it carefully under the tree, shivering slightly in the cool night air. Then she closed her eyes and reached for the fish that she had never dared touch before. It swam into her hands and lay there silently in her fingers. She pulled it out of the pool, and it neither gasped for air nor moved but shimmered silently in the moonlight.

"Ah, fish," said Kaya. "Would that I were your mate, deep down in the abbess's pool." And she stroked the fish's damp head and, on a sudden notion, kissed it. "Farewell."

As she bent to put the fish on the cloak, it suddenly began to struggle and turn in her hands. She held it more firmly, but it kept struggling, and as it moved, it began to grow and change. Its scales sloughed off like little silver halos. Its tail cleaved in two. Its neck stretched and lengthened and on its head silken hair began to grow. It pulled free of her at last, a naked man.

55

Kaya leaped back and gave a little cry, and at her voice the sisters stirred in their cells and rose up by twos and threes. Kaya heard them coming to the convent garden, their steps sounding unnaturally loud in the stillness of the night.

Quickly Kaya bent down and picked up her cloak from beneath the tree and wrapped it around the man.

"Who are you?" she whispered, for his face was deep in the shadows.

But just as the nuns came to the garden, he turned his head and the moonlight fully lit his face.

"Kay!" she cried, and ran to his arms.

He smiled and embraced her but he said nothing in return. Though he was a man again, he still had no tongue to tell it.

A priest was summoned, and upon hearing their tale, married them at once by the pool with the old abbess nodding her agreement. So their promise was kept, and once they were joined in that holy place, the sorcerer and his magic could not come between them.

Kay never regained his speech. But Kaya, who had grown used to the wordless ways of the convent, was content. And the silence they shared throughout their long and loving life together was as variously shaded as speech.

I woke up from a dream in which I had read out the first five paragraphs of this story. Of course I wrote them down. I have a notebook by the side of my bed just in case, though I rarely dream anything worthwhile.

Then, not knowing what the story was about, I let it sit in my infamous file drawer for months. Until my friend Mike Resnick sent me E-mail. "I am doing an anthology of witch stories," he said. "Do you have any unpublished?" Well, I knew I didn't have any unpublished stories. But I took out the folder of starts and this one leaped out at me. Of course! It was a witch story! Why hadn't I known that all along? The mind of a writer works (or doesn't work) in mysterious ways . . .

Circles

Peter Terwilliger drew a circle in the dirt, the circumference larger than his head. He drew an **X** in the center.

"There," he said. "Spit in it and make a wish. It'll come true."

I didn't believe him, of course. I might have been only seven years old, but I knew a thing or two. Spit didn't make wishes any more than it made polish. But I was sweet on Peter Terwilliger, who sat next to me in first grade, though I never showed it.

I spat and said, "I wish Old Man Johannson would die."

"Not out loud, stupid," Peter Terwilliger said, by which I knew he liked me.

Old Man Johannson didn't die, or at least not all at once. But he had a stroke that very night and spent the better part of a month drooling and staring at the wall. Enough time, in fact, for my father to get the money we needed to save our farm—Mama never dared ask him from where—and to pay off Old Man Johannson's heirs. They were just as mean as their father, tying the rest of the estate up in the courts for years. But Dad managed to sell our farm, poor as it was, for more than it was worth, and he moved us to the city.

I never saw Peter Terwilliger again.

In the city, Dad drank up all of the farm money and took to abusing Mama, first in small and then in big ways. He started by cursing her out, calling her down for her cooking or her mending or the dust under the bed. It progressed from there to pulling her hair and pinching her. One time he tripped her as she went by with a plate of mashed potatoes and she fell, breaking her arm. "It was an accident," she swore, and I believed her.

The night he beat her, however, was when I stopped believing. I could hear her trying to keep his voice and her cries low enough so as not to wake me or the neighbors. I got out of bed and trundled downstairs, not even bothering to put on my shoes or coat, though it was colder than a mine shaft outside.

I drew a circle in the dirt of an empty lot next door, bigger around than Peter Terwilliger's head, or what I remembered of it. Then I drew an X in the center.

"Make Dad leave Mama alone," I said, and spat.

He left her the next night for a blowsy waitress at the bar he frequented. It wasn't quite what I had had in mind.

Mama never recovered from his desertion and she never remarried. She raised me up alone.

It took a third wish to make me understand that my spit wishes worked, but they sure didn't go in circles. More like ellipses. Of course at seven and then at eight I didn't even know the word, much less its meaning. But I understood enough that I didn't make any more spit wishes for years.

When I was sixteen and mad at the world, but in particular at Mama, who was stricter than anyone else's mother, a spit wish I made when I was drunk with friends at a school dance led me to the understanding of this odd power I had.

Between Jemmy Sanders and Stephen Gallagher and Curtis Bast and me, we had downed a fifth of vodka. Jemmy and Curtis had gotten sick and Stephen had more or less passed out, making us wonder how we were going to get home since he was the only one old enough for a license or a car. The vodka just made me extraordinarily happy and loose.

"Car?" I said. "We don't need no stinking car. I'm a witch. I've got magic."

"Pumpkins?" mumbled Jemmy, in between bouts of puking. "You gonna turn a pumpkin into a coach?"

"Even better," I said. "Just you watch." I drew a circle bigger than Peter Terwilliger's head. Bigger even than his head would have been at sixteen. I drew an X in the center. Okay—it was a bit wobbly. So was I. But it was a recognizable X. Then I leaned over and spat in it.

"Cool," said Curtis.

"Gross," said Jemmy, and she promptly threw up again, well outside the circumference of the circle.

I laughed. "I wish we had a ride," I said.

At that very moment a police car pulled up next to us. In it was Haps Parker, the town constable and Stephen's stepfather. He waited until Jemmy and Curtis were through being sick. He waited until I stopped giggling. He slapped Stephen two or three times to wake him, then took us to the clinic for coffee and a thorough evaluation.

"I can't let your mother see you like this," he said several times to

59

Stephen. Haps was actually a nice guy; Stephen's dad had been a falling-down drunk.

That's how we spent half the night in the clinic and that's where I first met Polly Bangs, a nurse and a *real* witch. And that's where I learned how to control my circles of magic. Quite a ride indeed.

Polly said the trick was in the spit, not the circle. All bodily fluids, actually, contain magic. As a nurse she had access to the lot of them: spit, blood, urine, etc. Of course not everyone could just spit or pee and wish, or we'd be neck deep in wishes. That was Polly's line, not mine. You had to be born with the talent, like me.

After she told me—cleaned up Jemmy and Curtis and Stephen and told me—a lot of things became clear. Like my not getting drunk. Like my good grades in school, even though I never studied. Like Stephen, the most popular and best-looking guy in the class, falling for me. I had wished those things and they had happened. Not wishes with a circle, but wishes nonetheless. I remembered the evening I had discovered how much I wanted Stephen and I sat in the bathroom and alternately cried and had the runs. And wished he liked me. Wished as hard as I could. And he did.

"You mean," I whispered to Polly, "that I can have *anything* I want just by wishing?"

She shook her head. "You can get anything you wish for, but it won't ever be exactly what you expect. You are untrained. Wishes don't go in easy circles. They go in ellipses."

"We studied those in algebra," I said, remembering suddenly that I hadn't studied very hard. "Made graphs and everything." I had gotten an A and learned nothing. "Besides, I do, too, get exactly what I want. I got Stephen." I looked fondly over at him. He was sitting at the table with Jemmy and Curtis and drinking coffee. The little lock of blond hair fell down over his forehead. I loved that lock. I really did. Even if he was a funny color, kind of green, at the moment.

Polly touched my hand gently and mumbled something, and Stephen seemed to age thirty years. It was as if I were sitting across a kitchen table from him and he was that same funny color, apologizing to me—once again—for getting drunk, and promising it wouldn't happen again. I looked down. My hands, folded on the table, were shaking. My wrists and arms were bruised. I shook my head and everything was the same as before. Only it wasn't. Suddenly I didn't want Stephen anymore. Not even a little.

"Ellipses," I whispered, sort of like underlining a word in a textbook to aid in remembering it. "Ellipses."

I went back to the clinic every weekend after that. My mom thought I was interested in becoming a nurse. Actually I was studying witchcraft with Polly. We borrowed slides of blood samples from patients, which I studied under the microscope to learn about identifying witches. Witches' blood makes more white cells. Taken to the hospital, we are thought to be leukemic. Treated, we get sicker. Unless we are treated by a witch doctor.

Okay I laughed the first time I heard that, too. But Polly made sure I got to know the names of those doctors who were witches themselves, and who worked locally. She made sure my name got on the master list so they would know me as well.

And then, after I understood all the background, she taught me how to work on my wishes.

I would never be able to make them less elliptical. That's the nature of wishes. But I did learn how to anticipate the worst of the results. That way I could change the actual wording of the wish or decide not to make the wish at all.

61

I got good and I got older.

I studied with Polly all the way through high school and then decided to study medicine in college. I became a doctor and used my talent to help good folk get well. Bad folk—well, I just left them to their bodies' own devices.

And then one day—it was June 17—a man was brought into the emergency room where I was working. He was pretty badly torn up; his color and general state of wear and tear made me recognize him as a drunk. He had been a big man once but age and other stuff had shrunk him down like one of those apples off the tree.

But I knew him. Hadn't seen him since I was a kid, but I knew him. A witch knows her own.

"Hello, Dad," I whispered. His eyes widened but he was much too sick to answer back. I took his vital signs. They weren't good at all. My guess was he had next to no liver function left. I patched him up and stitched him up. I did everything that medicine could do, which wasn't enough.

He had just enough strength to grab my wrist. "Want a drink . . ." he murmured.

I closed the white curtains around us, cocooning us from the rest of the world. I stared down at him for a long while.

"Do it for me," he begged.

I drew a circle around his head on the gurney with my finger. I put a little cross on the right side, just by his ear. Not necessary, I knew, but the memories of that child in the cold empty lot were suddenly quite strong.

"Dad," I said slowly, "I wish you wouldn't die." Then, knowing no one could see us with the white curtains closed, I spat—very accurately—onto his forehead.

He cried out once and closed his eyes. He didn't even have the

strength to wipe away the spit, but lay there still as death. I watched as my spit dried on his skin, as his skin turned cool, then cold.

I opened the white curtains at last and went to the next patient, a child who had broken her arm. It was a quick and easy fix, and we traded knock-knock jokes all the while I was plastering the thing.

Dad lingered for fifteen years that way, floating in and out of consciousness, full of needles, full of pain, not alive, not dead.

Mama visited him once out of memory and once out of mercy, and never again.

At the hospital he was a kind of mascot and a kind of teaching tool. He lasted the entire time I was there. When I retired, I let him go, pulling the witching plug. I was the only mourner at his funeral.

At night I dream of him, large and still and cold and not quite dead. I expect I always will.

Ellipses.

My best friend in high school (who is now a well-known actress) and I used to read plays together aloud. In particular we were fond of the witches' scene from Macbeth. We did it brilliantly and with great gusto. Her younger brother made the sound effects, blowing through a straw into a soda bottle full of water, making the lines "Double, double, toil and trouble, Fire burn and cauldron bubble" sound realistic. I loved going over to her house. What I was totally unaware of at the time—and what she had been sworn to silence about—was that her parents were both alcoholics and suicidal. Her father managed to kill himself several years later. Only when she finally wrote a book about it, breaking out of that imposed silence, did she begin to heal. And only then did I understand what had been going on behind the walls of that pleasant house when visitors weren't around.

Weird Sisters

These are not women
with the healer's art,
these are not women
in face or heart,
but sisters of the night,
the deepest dark,
who speak in lightning
and light the spark
of mischief, murder;
they raise the flood
of deeds abhorrent,
steeped in wine, in blood.

We trembled, playing
at the game
of Hecate calling
Macbeth by name.
While all around
your house, a curse
more vivid than
Shakespearean verse
lay steeped in words
you dared not say,
until at last
you got away.

And there was I,
so deaf to rhyme,
I could not safe you
at the time
but played at witchcraft:
"Foul is fair . . ."
without a clue
to what lay there
in your white house
between the acts.
For fair *is* foul
when foul are facts.

During the course of putting together a big book called Favorite Folk Tales *from Around the World, I read more than five thousand stories from cultures all over our planet. Among my favorites were stories from the Native American traditions.*

One in particular, the Cheyenne story of an Arapaho slave who saves a young Cheyenne woman from brutal Crow masters, appealed to me. I found it first in George Bird Grinnell's By Cheyenne Campfires, *under the name of "The Bear Helper." I love not only the echoes of Cinderella in the story but the straightforward, unsentimental way it is told. I have tried to get that same voice into this story, along with a modern child's commentary. The boy in this story, like many contemporary children, is more familiar with stories like Cinderella than with his own culture's traditions.*

All cultures recognize people of power. Sometimes they are called witches, sometimes wizards, and sometimes, as in this story, they are shapeshifting shamans. In most places they are revered and—almost always—to some extent they are feared.

The Woman Who Loved a Bear

It was early in the autumn, the leaves turning over yellow in the puzzling wind, that a woman of the Cheyennes and her father went to collect meat he had killed. They each rode a horse and led a packhorse behind, for the father had killed two fine antelopes and had left them skinned and cut up and covered well with hide.

They didn't know that a party of Crows had found the cache and knew it for a Cheyenne kill by the hide covering it.

"We will wait for the hunter to come and collect his meat," they said. "We will get both a Cheyenne *and* his meat." They laughed at the thought.

And so it happened. The Cheyenne man and his daughter came innocently to the meat and the Crows charged down on them. The man was killed and his daughter was taken away as a prisoner, well to the north, to a village on the Sheep River, which is now called the Bighorn.

Is that the end of the story, Grandfather?

It is only the beginning. This is called "The Woman Who Loved a Bear." I have not even come to the bear yet.

The man who carried the pipe of the Crow war party was named Fifth Man Over and he had two wives. But when he looked at the Cheyenne girl he thought that she was very fine looking and wanted her for his wife. Of course his two wives were both Crow women, which means they were ugly and hard. They were not pleased about the Cheyenne woman becoming his third wife. When they asked her name, she told them she was called Walks with the Sun, so they called her Flat Foot Walker. But they could call her what they wanted, it did not change the fact that she was beautiful and they were not.

So whenever Fifth Man Over was away from the lodge, they abused the Cheyenne girl. They hit her with quirts and sticks and stones till her arms and legs were bruised. But they were careful not to hit her in the face, where even Fifth Man Over would see and ask questions.

The days and weeks went by and the beautiful Cheyenne wife had to do all the hard work. She had to pack the wood and dress the hides; she had to make moccasins, not only for her Crow husband, but for his ugly wives as well.

Grandfather, I have heard this story before. I have seen a movie of it. It is called "Cinderella."

Is there a bear in "Cinderella"?

No, of course not.

Then you do not know this story. This is a true story, from the time when children played games suited to their years and spoke with respect to their grandfathers. You will listen carefully so that you can tell the story just as I tell it to you.

Now, in Fifth Man Over's lodge there also lived a young man, about a year older than the Cheyenne woman, who was an Arapaho and had been taken as a slave in a raid when he was a small child. He had the keeping and herding of Fifth Man Over's horses. He was not straight and tall like a Cheyenne but limped, because his left foot had been burned in the raid that made him a slave. But he had a strong nose and straight black hair and he spoke softly to the Cheyenne woman.

"These women abuse you," he said. "You must not let them do so."

"I cannot do otherwise," Walks with the Sun answered. "They are my husband's elder wives." It was the proper answer, but she was a Cheyenne woman and they were only Crows, and so she said it through set teeth.

"Make many moccasins," the Arapaho told her. "Many more than are needed. Hide some away for yourself."

"Why should I do this?" she asked.

"Because you will need them on the trail back to your people."

She looked straight in his face and saw that there was no deceit there. She did not look at his crooked leg.

"You will wear out many moccasins on the trail," he said.

When does the bear come in, Grandfather?

Soon.

69

How soon?

Soon enough. It is not time to cut this story off. Listen. You will have to tell it back to me, you know.

Walks with the Sun made many moccasins and of every three she made, she hid one away. This took her through winter and into the spring, when the snow melted and the first flowers appeared down by the riverbank.

"We will go in the morning for the buffalo," said Fifth Man Over to his wives. By this he meant he would ride a horse and they would come behind with a packhorse pulling the travois sled.

"She should not come with us," said his first wife, pointing to Walks with the Sun. "She is a Cheyenne and has no stamina and will not be able to keep up and will want more than her share of the meat."

"And she is ugly," said the second wife, but she did not say it very loud.

"I will stay home, my husband," said Walks with the Sun, "and make the lodge ready for your return."

"And you will not break any of the pots we have worked so hard on," said the first wife.

"And you will not eat anything till we come back," said the second wife.

With all this Walks with the Sun agreed, though she would have loved to see the buffalo in their great herds and the men on their horses charging down on the bulls, even though they were Crow and not Cheyenne. She had heard that the sound of the buffalo running was like thunder on the great open plain, that it was a music that made the grasses dance. But she kept her head bent and her eyes modestly down.

So Fifth Man Over and his two wives and most of the other hunters and their wives left to go after the buffalo. And the Arapaho went, too, for he was to take care of the horses along the way

> *Grandfather, a buffalo is not a bear, and you promised.*
> *There will be a bear.*
> *Buffalo do not eat bear. Bear eat buffalo. I prefer the bear.*
> *There will be a bear.*
> *There had better be.*

But the young man returned the long way around, leaving his own horse in the timber outside of the camp. He came limping into the Crow village and the old people said to him, "Why are you here? What has happened to the people?" By this they meant the Crows.

"Nothing has happened to the people. They are following the buffalo. But my horse threw me and ran away and I have come back for another." He went to Fifth Man Over's lodge and saddled another horse and put two fine blankets on it, but not the best, because he was a slave after all. But before he mounted up, he went into the lodge and said to Walks with the Sun, "Now is your time. I have hidden my own horse in the timber down by the creek. You must take a large pot and go down as if for water and you will find it there. Put your extra moccasins in the pot, for should you lose the horse, you will surely need them."

"What of you?" asked Walks with the Sun. "Surely you want to leave here."

"I have no other home," he answered.

"Then you shall come home with me," she said.

"I am poor and I have a bad leg and I am not a Cheyenne," he said. "But I will watch out for you, never fear."

He rode away, but in a different direction from the creek, so that no one would suspect that the two of them had spoken. And Walks with the Sun did as he instructed. Taking a large pot, she put the moccasins in. Then she went to the creek. There she found the horse, saddled, with two blankets. Swinging herself up into the saddle, she began to ride south, toward her home.

I am still waiting, Grandfather.
Patience is a good thing in the young.
I am not patient. I am impatient.
I did not notice. The bear, though, is coming. In fact, Grandson, the bear is here.
Here? Where?
In the story. But you cannot see it unless you listen.
I see with my eyes. I hear with my ears, Grandfather.
You must do both, child. You must do both.

Walks with the Sun rode many miles, until both she and the horse were tired. So she got off, unsaddled it, and let the horse feed on the new spring grass. Then she resaddled the horse and rode another long time, past the Pumpkin Buttes. There she made camp, but without a fire, in case anyone should be looking for her.

In the middle of the night she awoke because of a huffing and snuffling sound and the horse got frightened and screamed like a white woman in labor, and broke its rope. It ran off, not to be found again.

And there, near here, with the moonlight on its back, was . . .

The bear, Grandfather.
The bear, Grandson.

Walks with the Sun spoke softly to the bear, not out of honor but out of fear. "O Bear," she said, "take pity on me. I am only a poor

Cheyenne woman and I am trying to get back to my own people." And then, quietly, carefully, she pulled on a pair of moccasins and stood. Carrying several more pairs in each hand, she backed away from the bear. When she could no longer see the great beast, she turned around and ran.

She ran until she was exhausted and then she turned and looked behind her. There was the bear, just a little way behind. So, taking a deep breath, she ran again, until she could barely put one foot in front of the other. When she turned to look again, the bear was still there.

At last she was so tired that she knew she must rest, even if the bear was to kill her. She sat down on a hollow log and fell asleep sitting up, heedless of the bear.

While she slept, she heard the bear speak to her. His voice was like the rocks in a river, with the water rushing over. He said, "Get up and go to your people. I am watching to protect you. I am stepping in your tracks so that the Crows cannot trail you, so that Fifth Man Over and his ugly wives cannot find you."

When Walks with the Sun awoke, it was still dark. The bear was squatting on its haunches not far from her, its head crowned with the stars. Awake, she did not think he could have spoken, so she was still afraid of him.

She rose carefully, put on new moccasins, and began her journey again, but this time she did not run. She walked on until she could walk no longer. Then she lay down under a tree and slept.

You said he spoke in a dream, Grandfather.
I said he spoke while she slept, Grandson.
Is that the same as really *speaking?*
You are sitting with me on the buffalo-calf robe. Do you need to ask such questions?

———

74

In the morning Walks with the Sun awoke and saw the bear a little way off on top of a small butte. It did not seem to be looking at her, but when she started to walk, it followed again in her tracks.

So it went all the day, till she reached the Platte River. Since this was early spring, the waters were full from bank to bank. Walks with the Sun had no idea how she could get across.

She sighed out loud but said nothing else. At the sound, the bear came over to her, looked in her face, and his breath was hot and foul smelling. Then he turned his back to her and stuck his great rear in her face. By this she knew that he wanted her to get on his back.

"Bear," she said, "if you are willing to take me across the river, I am willing to ride." And she crawled on his back and put her arms around his neck, just in front of his mighty shoulders.

With a snort, he plunged into the water.

The water was cold. She could feel it through her leggings. And the river tumbled strongly over its rocky bed. But stronger still was the bear, and he swam across with ease.

When they got to the other side, the bear waited while she dismounted, then he shook himself all over, scattering water on every leaf and stone. Then he rolled on the ground.

While he was rolling, Walks with the Sun started on. When she looked back, the bear was following her just as he had before.

So it went for many days, the Cheyenne woman walking, the bear coming along behind. When she was hungry, he caught a young buffalo calf and killed it. She skinned it, cut it into pieces, took her flint and made a fire, then cooked the meat. Some of it she ate, and some she gave to the bear. The rest she rolled in the skin, making a pack that she carried on her back.

Did she feed him by hand, Grandfather?
By hand?

75

Did she hold pieces for him to eat?

That would be foolish, indeed, Grandson. He could have taken her hand off at the wrist and not even noticed. Where do you young people come up with such foolish ideas, heh?

Then how did she feed the bear?

She put it down on the ground a little way from the bear, and he walked up and ate it.

Oh.

They came at last to the Laramie River and below was a big village, with so many lodges they covered the entire bank.

"I do not know if those are my people or not," Walks with the Sun said. "Can you go and find out for me?"

The bear went up close to the outermost lodge, but someone saw him and shouted and someone else, an old man whose hand was not so steady, shot an arrow at him. The arrow pierced his left hind foot and he ran back to Walks with the Sun, limping.

"O Bear," she cried, "you are hurt and it is all my fault." She knelt down and pulled the arrow from his foot and stopped the bleeding with the heel of her hand.

When the people tracked the blood trail to them, she was still sitting there, holding the bear in her arms. Only he was no longer a bear, but a young man with a strong nose and straight black hair and a left foot that was not quite straight.

The bear turned into the Arapaho slave, Grandfather?

That is not what I said, Grandson.

But I thought you said . . .

Listen, Grandson, listen.

Walks with the Sun took the buffalo hide, shook it out, and turned it so the hair side was outward. Then she wrapped the Arapaho in it

to show he was a medicine man. Her people put great strings of beads around his neck and gave him feathers to honor him. Then they lifted him onto a travois sled and, pulling it themselves, brought him into the village.

He never walked as a bear again, except twice, when the people were threatened by Crows. Walks with the Sun became his wife and they had many children and many grandchildren, of which I am one, and you are another. The buffalo hide we are sitting on today is the very one of which I have spoken.

Is that a true story, Grandfather?

It is a true story, Grandson.

But how can it be true, Grandfather? People can't turn into bears. Bears can't turn into people.

Heh. They do not do so today. But we are speaking of the time when the Cheyennes were a great nation and still in the north, when the land was covered with buffalo, and we passed the medicine arrows and buffalo hat from keeper to keeper.

And the buffalo hide, Grandfather?

And the buffalo hide, Grandson. This ties it off.

What does that mean?

That storytelling is over for the night. That it is time for children to ask no more questions but to sleep. For old men to dream by the fire.

This ties it off, Grandfather.

I collect old children's books and illustrated books from the nineteenth and early twentieth centuries. One of the volumes I purchased at a street fair in Edinburgh, Scotland, was The Queen's Book of the Red Cross. *In it was a delightful verse by J. B. Morton called "A Love Song." It begins, "When love comes to the harbour-master . . ." and is all about the havoc wreaked upon the town while he tosses upon his bed writing silly verses to some girl. You can see how this inspired me.*

Witch Alfre is named after Alfre Woodard, one of my favorite actresses. "Widdershins" is a counterclockwise direction, often used in magical spells. Amanita is a poisonous mushroom.

When Love Came
to Witch Alfre

When love came to Witch Alfre
She sat all day sighing,
Little caring the cat was not fed
And the amanita dying.

When love came to Witch Alfre
She took to her bed dejected.
The cauldron went unstirred and cold;
The herbs stayed uncollected.

When love came to Witch Alfre
Everyone in town knew
From the awful smell that arose
From her unattended brew.

When love came to Witch Alfre
Life went widdershins motion,
Till a friend from town came out
And made an anti-love potion.

Perhaps the most famous wizard of all—at least in Western cultures—is Merlin, who served King Arthur. I have been fascinated by the figure of Merlin ever since I was a child. Of all the characters in the King Arthur stories, he is my favorite. I have written a book of stories about him, Merlin's Booke, from which this one is taken. I have written a picture book about him—Merlin and the Dragons, which was made into a film. I have written a short novel about him as an old man: The Dragon's Boy. And I am working on a trilogy I call the Young Merlin trilogy, comprised of the books Passager, Hobby, and Merlin, all terms from falconry.

He sneaks into my tales, my novels, my poems, my songs—and my dreams. Wizardry indeed.

The Sword and the Stone

"Would you believe a sword in a stone, my liege?" the old necromancer asked. "I dreamed of one last night. Stone white as whey with a sword stuck in the top like a knife through butter. It means something. My dreams always mean something. Do you believe that stone and that sword, my lord?"

The man on the carved wooden throne sighed heavily, his breath causing the hairs of his moustache to flap. "Merlinnus, I have no time to believe in a sword in a stone. Or on a stone. Or under a stone. I'm just too damnably tired for believing today. And you *always* have dreams."

"This dream is different, my liege."

"They're always different. But I've just spent half a morning pacifying two quarreling *dux dellorum.* Or is it *bellori?*"

"*Belli,*" muttered the mage, shaking his head.

"Whatever. And sorting out five counterclaims from my chief cook and his mistresses. He should stick to his kitchen. His affairs are a mess. And awarding grain to a lady whose miller maliciously killed her cat. Did you know, Merlinnus, that we actually have a law about cat killing that levies a fine of the amount of grain that will cover the dead cat completely when it is held up by the tip of its tail and its nose touches the ground? It took over a peck of grain." He sighed again.

"A large cat, my lord," mumbled the mage.

"A *very* large cat indeed," agreed the King, letting his head sink into his hands. "And a *very* large lady. With a lot of *very* large and important lands. Now what in Mithras's name do I want a sword and a stone for when I have to deal with all that?"

"In *Christ's* name, my lord. *Christ's* name. Remember, we are Christians now." The mage held up a gnarled forefinger. "And it is a sword *in* a stone."

"*You* are the Christian," the King said. "*I* still drink bull's blood with my men. It makes them happy, though the taste of it is somewhat less than good wine." He laughed mirthlessly. "And yet I wonder how good a Christian you are, Merlinnus, when you still insist on talking to trees. Oh, there are those who have seen you walking in your wood and talking, always talking, even though there is no one there. Once a Druid, always a Druid, so Sir Kai says."

"Kai is a fool," answered the old man, crossing himself quickly, as if marking the points of the body punctuated his thought.

"Kai is a fool, indeed, but even fools have ears and eyes. Go away, Merlinnus, and do not trouble me with this sword on a stone. I have more important things to deal with." He made several dismissing movements with his left hand while summoning the next petitioner with his right. The petitioner, a young woman with a saucy smile and a bodice bouncing with promises, moved forward. The King smiled back.

Merlinnus left and went outside, walking with more care than absolutely necessary, to the grove beyond the castle walls where his favorite oak grew. He addressed it rather informally, they being of a long acquaintance.

"*Salve, amice frondifer,* greetings, friend leaf bearer. What am I to do with that boy? When I picked him out it was because the blood of a strong-minded and lusty king ran in his veins, though on the sinister side. Should I then have expected gratitude and imagination to accompany such a heritage? Ah, but unfortunately I did. My brains must be rotting away with age. Tell me, *e glande nate,* sprout of an acorn, do I ask too much? Vision! That's what is missing, is it not?"

A rustle of leaves, as if a tiny wind puzzled through the grove, was his only answer.

Merlinnus sat down at the foot of the tree and rubbed his back against the bark, easing an itch that had been there since breakfast. He tucked the skirt of his woolen robe between his legs and stared at his feet. He still favored the Roman summer sandals, even into late fall, because closed boots tended to make the skin between his toes crackle like old parchment. And besides, in the heavy boots, his feet sweated and stank. But he always felt cold now, winter and summer. So he wore a woolen robe year round.

"Did I address him incorrectly, do you think? These new kings are such sticklers for etiquette. An old man like me finds that stuff boring. Such a waste of time, and time is the one commodity I have little of." He rubbed a finger alongside his nose.

"I thought to pique his interest, to get him wondering about a sword that is stuck in a stone like a knife in a slab of fresh beef. A bit of legerdemain, that, and I'm rather proud of it actually. You see, it wasn't *just* a dream. I've done it up in my tower room. Anyone with a bit of knowledge can read the old Latin building manuals and construct a ring of stones. Building the baths under the castle was harder work. But that sword in the stone—yes, I'm rather proud of it. And what that young king has got to realize is that he needs to do something more than rule on cases of quarreling dukes and petty mistresses and grasping rich widows. He has to . . ." Stopping for a minute to listen to the wind again through trees, Merlinnus shook his head and went on. "He has to fire up these silly tribes, give them something magical to rally them. I don't mean him to be just another petty chieftain. Oh, no. He's to be my greatest creation, that boy." He rubbed his nose again. "My last creation, I'm afraid. If this one doesn't work out, what am I to do?"

The wind, now stronger, soughed through the trees.

"I was given just thirty-three years to bind this kingdom, you know. That's the charge, the geas laid on me: thirty-three years to bind it *per crucem et quercum,* by cross and by oak. And this, alas, is the last year."

A cuckoo called down from the limb over his head.

"The first one I tried was that idiot Uther. Why, his head was more wood than thine." The old man chuckled to himself. "And then there were those twins from the Hebrides who enjoyed games so much. Then that witch, Morgana. She made a pretty mess of things. I even considered—at her prompting—her strange, dark little son. Or was he her nephew? I forget which. When one has been a lifelong celibate as I, one tends to dismiss such frequent and casual couplings and their messy aftermaths as unimportant. But that boy had a sly, foxy look about him. Nothing would follow him but a pack of dogs. And then I found this one right under my nose. In some ways he's the dullest of the lot, and yet in a king dullness can be a virtue. *If* the crown is secure."

A nut fell on his head, tumbled down his chest, and landed in his lap. It was a walnut, which was indeed strange, since he was sitting beneath an oak. Expecting magic, the mage looked up. There was a little red squirrel staring down at him. Merlinnus cracked the nut between two stones, extracted the meat, and held up half to the squirrel.

"Walnuts from acorn trees," he said. As soon as the squirrel had snatched away its half of the nutmeat, the old man drifted off into a dream-filled sleep.

"Wake up, wake up, old one." It was the shaking, not the sentence, that woke him. He opened his eyes. A film of sleep lent a soft focus to his vision. The person standing over him seemed haloed in mist.

"Are you all right, Grandfather?" The voice was soft, too.

Merlinnus sat up. He was, he guessed, too old to be sleeping out of doors. The ground cold had seeped into his bones. Like an old tree, his sap ran sluggishly. But being caught out by a youngster made him grumpy. "Why shouldn't I be all right?" he answered, more gruffly than he meant.

"You are so thin, Grandfather, and you sleep so silently. I feared you dead. One should not die in a sacred grove. It offends the Goddess."

"Are you then a worshiper of the White One?" he asked, carefully watching the stranger's hands. No true worshiper would answer that question in a straightforward manner, but would instead signal the dark secret with an inconspicuous semaphore. But all that the fingers signed were concern for him. Forefinger, fool's finger, physic's finger, ear finger were silent of secrets. Merlinnus sighed and struggled to sit upright.

The stranger put a hand under his arm and back and gently eased him into a comfortable position. Once up, Merlinnus took a better look. The stranger was a boy with that soft lambent cheek not yet coarsened by a beard. His eyes were the clear blue of speedwells. The eyebrows were dark swallow wings, sweeping high and back toward luxuriant and surprisingly gold hair caught under a dark cap. He was

dressed in homespun but neat and clean. His hands, clasped before him, were small and well formed.

Sensing the mage's inspection, the boy spoke. "I have come in the hopes of becoming a page at court." Then he added, "I wish to learn the sword and lance."

Merlinnus's mouth screwed about a bit but at last settled into a passable smile. Perhaps he could find some use for the boy. A wedge properly placed had been known to split a mighty tree. And he had so little time. "What is your name, boy?"

"I am called . . ." There was a hesitation, scarcely noticeable. "Gawen."

Merlin's smile broadened. "Ah, but we have already a great knight by a similar name. He is praised as one of the king's Three Fearless Men."

"Fearless in bed, certainly," the boy answered. "The hollow man." Then, as if to soften his words, he added, "Or so it is said where I come from."

So, Merlinnus thought, *there may be more to this than a child come to court.* Aloud, he said, "And where *do* you come from?"

The boy looked down and smoothed the homespun where it lay against his thighs. "The coast."

Refusing to comment that the coast was many miles long, both north and south, Merlinnus said sharply, "Do not condemn a man with another's words. And do not praise him that way, either."

The boy did not answer.

"Purity in tongue must precede purity in body," the mage added, for the boy's silence annoyed him. "That is my first lesson to you."

A small sulky voice answered him. "I am too old for lessons."

"None of us is too old," said Merlinnus, wondering why he felt so compelled to go on and on. Then, as if to soften his criticism, he added, "Even I learned something today."

"And that is . . . ?"

"It has to do with the Matter of Britain," the mage said, "and is therefore beyond you."

"Why beyond me?"

"Give me your hand." He held his own out, crabbed with age.

Gawen reluctantly put his small hand forward, and the mage ran a finger across the palm, slicing the lifeline where it forked early.

"I see you are no stranger to work. The calluses tell me that. But what work it is I do not know."

Gawen withdrew his hand and smiled brightly, his mouth wide, mobile, telling of obvious relief.

Merlinnus wondered what other secrets the hand might have told him, could he have read palms as easily as a village herb wife. Then, shaking his head, he stood.

"Come. Before I bring you into court, let us go and wash ourselves in the river."

The boy's eyes brightened. "*You* can bring me to court?"

With more pride than he felt and more hope than he had any right to feel, Merlinnus smiled. "Of course, my son. After all, I am the High King's mage."

They walked companionably to the river, which ran noisily between stones. Willows on the bank wept their leaves into the swift current. Merlinnus used the willow trunks for support as he sat down carefully on the bank. He eased his feet, sandals and all, into the cold water. It was too fast and too slippery for him to stand.

"Bring me enough to bathe with," he said, pointing to the water. It could be a test of the boy's quick-wittedness.

Gawan stripped off his cap, knelt down, and held the cap in the river. Then he pulled it out and wrung the water over the old man's hands.

Merlinnus liked that. The job had been done, and quickly, with little wasted motion. Another boy might have plunged into the river, splashing like an untrained animal. Or asked what to do.

The boy muttered, *"De matro ad patri."*

Startled, Merlinnus looked up into the clear, untroubled blue eyes. "You know Latin?"

"Did I . . . did I say it wrong?"

"'From the mother to the father.'"

"That is what I meant." Gawen's young face was immediately transformed by the wide smile. "The . . . the brothers taught me."

Merlinnus knew of only two monasteries along the coast and they were both very far away. The sisters of Quintern Abbey were much closer, but they never taught boys. *This child*, thought the mage, *has come a very long way indeed*. Aloud, he said, "They taught you well."

Gawen bent down again, dipped the cap once more, and this time used the water to wash his own face and hands. Then he wrung the cap out thoroughly but did not put it back on his head. Cap in hand, he faced the mage. "You *will* bring me to the High King, then?"

A sudden song welled up in Merlinnus's breast, a high hallelujah so unlike any of the dark chantings he was used to under the oaks. "I will," he said.

As they neared the castle, the sun was setting. It was unusually brilliant, rain and fog being the ordinary settings for evenings in early fall. The high tor, rumored to be hollow, was haloed with gold and loomed up behind the topmost towers.

Gawen gasped at the high timbered walls.

Merlinnus smiled to himself but said nothing. For a child from the coast, such walls must seem near miraculous. But for the competent architect who planned for eternity, mathematics was miracle enough.

He had long studied the writing of the Roman builders, whose prose styles were as tedious as their knowledge was great. He had learned from them how to instruct men in the slotting of breastwork timbers. All he had needed was the ability to read—and time. Yet time, he thought bitterly, for construction as with everything else, had all but run out for him. Still, there was this boy—and this *now*.

"Come," said the mage. "Stand tall and enter."

The boy squared his shoulders, and boy and mage hammered upon the carved wooden doors together.

Having first checked them out through the spyhole, the guards opened the doors with a desultory air that marked them at the end of their watch.

"*Ave* Merlinnus," said one guard with an execrable accent. It was obvious he knew that much Latin and no more. The other guard was silent.

Gawen was silent as well, but his small silence was filled with wonder. Merlinnus glanced slantwise and saw the boy taking in the great stoneworks, the Roman mosaic panel on the entry wall, all the fine details he had insisted upon. He remembered the argument with Morgana when they had built that wall.

"An awed emissary," he had told her, "is already half won over."

At least she had had the wit to agree, though later those same wits had been addled by drugs and wine and the gods only knew what other excesses. Merlinnus shook his head. It was best to look forward, not back, when you had so little time. Looking backward was an old man's drug.

He put his hand on the boy's shoulder, feeling the fine bones beneath the jerkin. "Turn here," he said softly.

They turned into the long, dark walkway where the walls were niched for the slide of three separate portcullises. No invaders could break in this way. Merlinnus was proud of the castle's defenses.

91

As they walked, Gawen's head was constantly aswivel: left, right, up, down. Wherever he had come from had left him unprepared for this. At last the hall opened into an inner courtyard where pigs, poultry, and wagons vied for space.

Gawen breathed out again. "It's like home," he whispered.

"Eh?" Merlinnus let out a whistle of air like a skin bag deflating.

"Only finer, of course." The quick answer was almost satisfying, but not quite. Not quite. And Merlinnus was not one to enjoy unsolved puzzles.

"To the right," the old man growled, shoving his finger hard into the boy's back. "To the right."

They were ushered into the throne room without a moment's hesitation. This much, at least, a long memory and a reputation for magic-making and king-making brought him.

The King looked up from the paper he was laboriously reading, his finger marking his place. He always, Merlinnus noted with regret, read well behind that finger, for he had come to reading as a grown man, and reluctantly, his fingers faster in all activities than his mind. But he *was* well meaning, the mage reminded himself. Just a bit sluggish on the uptake. A king should be faster than his advisors, though he seem to lean upon them; quicker than his knights, though he seem to send them on ahead.

"Ah, Merlinnus, I am glad you are back. There's a dinner tonight with an emissary from the Orkneys and you know I have trouble understanding their rough mangling of English. You will be there?"

Merlinnus nodded.

"And there is a contest I need your advice on. Here." He snapped his fingers and a list was put into his hand. "The men want to choose a May Queen to serve next year. I think they are hoping to thrust her on me as my queen. They have drawn up a list of those qualities they think she should possess. Kai wrote the list down."

Kai, Merlinnus thought disagreeably, was the only one of that crew who *could* write, and his spelling was only marginally better than his script. He took the list and scanned it:

Thre thingges smalle—headde, nose, breestes;
Thre thingges largge—waiste, hippes, calves;
Thre thingges longge—haires, finggers, thies;
Thre thingges short—height, toes, utterance.

"Sounds more like an animal in a bestiary than a girl, my lord," Merlinnus ventured at last.

Gawen giggled.

"They are trying . . ." the King began.

"They certainly are," muttered the mage.

"They are trying . . . to be helpful, Merlinnus." The King glowered at the boy by the mage's side. "And who is this fey bit of work?"

The boy bowed deeply. "I am called Gawen, Sire, and I have come to learn to be a knight."

The King ground his teeth. "And some of them, no doubt, will like you be-nights."

A flush spread across the boy's cheeks. "I am sworn to the Holy Mother to be pure," he said.

"Are you a Grailer or a Goddess worshiper?" Before the boy could answer, the King turned to Merlinnus. "Is he well bred?"

"Of course," said Merlinnus, guessing. The Latin and the elegant speech said as much, even without the slip about how much a castle looked like home.

"Very well," the King said, arching his back and putting one hand behind him. "Damned throne's too hard. I think I actually prefer a soldier's pallet. Or a horse." He stood and stretched. "That's enough for one day. I will look at the rest tomorrow." He put out a hand and

93

steadied himself, using the mage's shoulder, then descended the two steps to the ground.

Speaking into Merlinnus's right ear because he knew the left ear was a bit deafened by age, the King said, "When you gave me the kingdom, you forgot to mention that kings need to sit all day long. You neglected to tell me about wooden thrones. If you had told me that when you offered me the crown, I might have thought about it a bit longer."

"And would you have made a different choice, my lord?" asked Merlinnus quietly.

The King laughed and said aloud, "No, but I would have requested a different throne."

Merlinnus looked shocked. "But that is the High King's throne. Without it, you would not be recognized."

The King nodded.

Gawen, silent until this moment, spoke up. "Would not a cushion atop the throne do? Like the crown atop the High King's head?"

The King's hand went immediately to the heavy circlet of metal on his head. Then he swept it off, shook out his long blond locks, and laughed. "Of course. A cushion. Out of the mouth of babes . . . It would do, would it not, Merlinnus?"

The mage's mouth twisted about the word. "Cushion." But he could think of no objection. It was the quiet homeyness of the solution that offended him. But certainly it would work.

Merlinnus put aside his niggling doubts about the boy Gawen and turned instead to the problem at hand: making the King accept the magic of the sword in the stone.

"I beg you, Sire," the old mage said the next morning, "to listen." He accompanied his request with a bow on bended knee. The pains of increasing age were only slightly mitigated by some tisanes brewed by a local herb wife. Merlinnus sighed heavily as he went down. It was that sigh, sounding so much like his old grandfather's, that decided the King.

"All right, all right, Merlinnus. Let us see this sword and this stone."

"It is in my workroom," Merlinnus said. "If you will accompany me there." He tried to stand and could not.

"I will not only accompany you," said the King patiently, "it looks as if I will have to carry you." He came down from his throne and lifted the old man up to his feet.

"I can walk," Merlinnus said somewhat testily.

Arm in arm, they wound through the castle halls, up three flights of stone stairs to Merlinnus's tower workroom.

The door opened with a spoken spell and three keys. The King seemed little impressed.

"*There!*" said the mage, pointing to a block of white marble with veins of red and green running through. Sticking out of the stone top was the hilt of a sword. The hilt was carved with wonderful runes. On the white marble face was the legend:

WHOSO PULLETH OUTE

THIS SWERD OF THIS STONE

IS RIGHTWYS KYNGE BORNE OF

ALL BRYTAYGNE

Slowly the King read aloud, his finger tracing the letters in the stone. When he had finished, he looked up. "But *I* am king of all Britain."

"Then pull the sword, Sire."

The King smiled and it was not a pleasant smile. He was a strong man, in his prime, and except for his best friend, Sir Lancelot, he was reputed to be the strongest in the kingdom. It was one of the reasons

Merlinnus had chosen him. He put his hand to the hilt, tightened his fingers around it until the knuckles were white, and pulled.

The sword remained in the stone.

"Merlinnus, this is witchery. I will not have it." The King's voice was cold.

"And with *witchery* you will pull it out, in full view of the admiring throngs. You—and no one else." The mage smiled benignly.

The King let go of the sword. "But why this? I am *already* king."

"Because I hear grumblings in the kingdom. Oh, do not look slant-wise at me, boy. It is not magic but reliable spies that tell me so. There are those who refuse to follow you, to be bound to you, and so bind this kingdom, because they doubt the legitimacy of your claim."

The King snorted. "And they are right, Merlinnus. I am king be-cause the archmage wills it. *Per crucem et quercum.*"

Startled, Merlinnus asked, "How did you know that?"

"Oh, my old friend, do you think you are the only one with reli-able spies?"

Merlinnus stared into the King's eyes. "Yes, you are right. You are king because I willed it. And because you earned it. But this bit of legerdemain . . ."

"Witchery!" interrupted the King.

Merlinnus persisted. "This *legerdemain* will have them all believing in you." He added quickly, "As I do. *All* of them. To bind the kingdom you need *all* the tribes to follow you."

The King looked down and then, as if free of the magic for a moment, turned and stared out of the tower window to the north, where winter was already creeping down the mountainsides. "Do those few tribes matter? The ones who paint themselves blue and squat naked around small fires? The ones who wrap themselves in woolen blankets and blow noisily into animal bladders, calling it song? The ones who dig out shelled fish with their toes and eat the fish raw?

Do we really want to bring them to our kingdom?"

"They are all part of Britain. The Britain of which you are the king now and for the future."

The King shifted his gaze from the mountains to the guards walking his donjon walls. "Are you positive I shall be able to draw the sword? I will *not* be made a mockery to satisfy some hidden purpose of yours."

"Put your hand on the sword, Sire."

The King turned slowly, as if the words had a power to command him. He walked back to the marble. It seemed to glow. He reached out and then, before his hand touched the hilt, by an incredible act of will, he stopped. "I am a good soldier, Merlinnus. And I love this land."

"I know."

With a resonant slap the King's hand grasped the sword. Merlinnus muttered something in a voice as soft as a cradle song. The sword slid noiselessly from the stone.

Holding the sword above his head, the King turned and looked steadily at the mage. "If I were a wicked man, I would bring this down on your head. Now."

"I know."

Slowly the sword descended, and when it was level with his eyes, the King put his left hand to the hilt as well. He hefted the sword several times and made soft comfortable noises deep in his chest. Then carefully, like a woman threading a needle, he slid the sword back into its slot in the stone.

"I will have my men take this and place it before the great cathedral so that all might see it. *All* my people shall have a chance to try their hands."

"All?"

"Even the ones who paint themselves blue or blow into bladders or do other disgusting and uncivilized things." The King smiled. "I shall even let mages try."

Merlinnus smiled back. "Is that wise?"

"I am the one with the strong arm, Merlinnus. You are to provide the wisdom. And the witchery."

"Then let the mages try, too," Merlinnus said. "For all the good it will do them."

"It is a fine sword, Merlinnus. It shall honor its wielder." He put his hand back on the hilt and heaved. The sword did not move.

The soldiers, with no help from Merlinnus, moaned and pushed and sweated and pulled until at last they managed to remove the sword-and-stone with a series of rollers and ropes. At the King's request it was set up in front of the great cathedral in the center of the town, outside the castle walls. News of it was carried by carters and jongleurs, gleemen and criers, from castle to castle and town to town. Within a month the hilt of the sword was filthy from the press of hundreds of hands. It seemed that in the countryside there were many who would be king.

Young Gawen took it upon himself to clean the hilt whenever he had time. He polished the runes on the stone lovingly, too, and studied the white marble from all angles. But he never put his hand to the sword as if to pull it. When the King was told of this, he smiled and his hand strayed to the cushion beneath him.

Gawen reported on the crowds around the stone to Merlinnus as he recounted his other lessons.

"Helm, aventail, byrnie, gauntlet, cuisses . . ." he recited, touching the parts of his body where the armor would rest. "And, archmage, there was a giant of a man there today, dressed all in black, who tried the sword. And six strange tribesmen with blue skin and necklaces of shells. Two of them tried to pull together. The sword would not come out, but their blue dye came off. I had a horrible time scrubbing it from the hilt. And Sir Kai came."

"Again?"

The boy laughed. "It was his sixth try. He waits until it is dinnertime and no one is in the square."

The old mage nodded at every word. "Tell me again."

"About Sir Kai?"

"About the parts of the armor. You must have the lesson perfect for tomorrow."

The boy's mouth narrowed as he began. "Helm, aventail . . ."

At each word, Merlinnus felt a surge of pride and puzzlement. Though the recitation was an old one, it sounded new and somehow different in Gawen's mouth.

They waited until the night of the solstice, when the earth sat poised between night and night. Great bonfires were lit in front of the cathedral to drive back the darkness, while inside candles were lighted to do the same.

"It is time," Merlinnus said to the King, without any preliminaries.

"It is always time," answered the King, placing his careful marks on the bottom of yet another piece of parchment.

"I mean time to pull the sword from the stone." Merlinnus offered his hand to the King.

Pushing aside the offer, the King rose.

"I see you use the cushion now," Merlinnus said.

"It helps somewhat." He stretched. "I only wish I had two of them."

The mage shook his head. "You are the King. Command the second."

The King looked at him steadily. "I doubt such excess is wise."

Remembering Morgana, the mage smiled.

99

They walked arm in arm to the waiting horses. Merlinnus was helped onto a grey whose broad back was more like a chair than a charger. But then, he had always been ill at ease on horseback. And horses, even the ones with the calmest dispositions, sensed some strangeness in him. They always shied.

The King strode to his own horse, a barrel-chested bay with a smallish head. It had been his mount when he was a simple soldier and he had resisted all attempts to make him ride another.

"Mount up," the King called to his guards.

Behind him his retinue mounted. Sir Kai was the first to vault into the saddle. Young Gawen, astride a pony that was a present from the King, was the last.

With a minimum of fuss, they wound along the path down the hillside toward the town, and only the clopping of hooves on dirt marked their passage. Ahead were torchbearers and behind them came the household, each with a candle. So light came to light, a wavering parade to the waiting stone below.

In the fire-broken night the white stone gleamed before the black hulk of the cathedral. The darker veins in the stone meandered like faery streams across its surface. The sword, now shadow, now light, was the focus of hundreds of eyes. And, as if pulled by some invisible string, the King rode directly to the stone, dismounted, and knelt before it. Then he removed his circlet of office and shook free the long golden mane it had held so firmly in place. When he stood again, he put the crown on the top of the stone so that it lay just below the angled sword.

The crowd fell still.

"This crown and this land belong to the man who can pull the sword from the stone," the King said, his voice booming into the

strange silence. "So it is written—here." He gestured broadly with his hand toward the runes.

"Read it," cried a woman's voice from the crowd.

"We want to hear it," shouted another.

A man's voice, picking up her argument, dared a further step. "We want the mage to read it." Anonymity lent his words power. The crowd muttered its agreement.

Merlinnus dismounted carefully and, after adjusting his robes, walked to the stone. He glanced only briefly at the words on its side, then turned to face the people.

"The message on the stone is burned here," he said, pointing to his breast, "here in my heart. It says, *Whoso pulleth out this sword of this stone is rightwise king born of all Britain.*"

Sir Kai nodded and said loudly, "Yes, that is what it says. Right."

The King put his hands on his hips. "And so, good people, the challenge has been thrown down before us all. He who would be king of all Britain must step forward and put his hand on the sword."

At first there was no sound at all but the dying echo of the King's voice. Then a child cried and that started the crowd. They began talking to one another, jostling, arguing, some good-naturedly and others with a belligerent tone. Finally, a rather sheepish farm boy, taller by almost a head than Sir Kai, who was the tallest of the knights, was thrust from the crowd. He had a shock of wheat-colored hair over one eye and a dimple in his chin.

"I'd try, my lord," he said. He was plainly uncomfortable, having to talk to the King. "I mean, it wouldn't do no harm."

"No harm indeed, son," said the King. He took the boy by the elbow and escorted him to the stone.

The boy put both his hands around the hilt and then stopped. He looked over his shoulder at the crowd. Someone shouted encouragement and then the whole push of people began to call out to him.

"Do it. Pull the bastard. Give it a heave. Haul it out." Their cries came thick now and, buoyed by their excitement, the boy put his right foot up against the stone. Then he leaned backward and pulled. His hands slipped along the hilt and he fell onto his bottom, to the delight of the crowd.

Crestfallen, the boy stood up. He stared unhappily at his worn boots, as if he did not know where else to look or how to make his feet carry him away.

The King put his hand on the boy's shoulder. "What is your name, son?" The gentleness in his voice silenced the crowd's laughter.

"Percy, sir," the boy managed at last.

"Then, Percy," said the King, "because you were brave enough to try where no one else would set hand on the sword, you shall come to the castle and learn to be one of my knights."

"Maybe not *your* knight," someone shouted from the crowd.

A shadow passed over the King's face and he turned toward the mage.

Merlinnus shook his head imperceptibly and put his finger to his lips.

The King shifted his gaze back to the crowd. He smiled. "No, perhaps not. We shall see. Who else would try?"

At last Sir Kai brushed his hand across his breastplate. He alone of the court still affected the Roman style. Tugging his gloves down so that the fingers fitted snugly, he walked to the stone and placed his right hand on the hilt. He gave it a slight tug, smoothed his golden moustache with the fingers of his left hand, then reached over with his left hand and with both gave a mighty yank. The sword did not move.

Kai shrugged and turned toward the King. "But I am still first in your service," he said.

"And in my heart, brother," acknowledged the King.

103

Then, one by one, the knights lined up and took turns pulling on the sword. Stocky Bedevere; handsome Gawain; Tristan, maned like a lion; cocky Galahad; and the rest. But the sword, ever firm in its stone scabbard, never moved.

At last, of all the court's knights, only Lancelot was left.

"And you, good Lance, my right hand, the strongest of us all, will you not try?" asked the King.

Lancelot, who disdained armor except in battle and was dressed in a simple tunic, the kind one might dance in, shook his head. "I have no wish to be king. I only wish to be of service."

The King walked over to him and put his hand on Lancelot's shoulder. He whispered into the knight's ear. "It is the stone's desire, not ours, that will decide this. But if you do *not* try, then my leadership will always be in doubt. Without your full commitment to this cause, the kingdom will not be bound."

"Then I will put my hand to it, my lord," Lancelot said. "Because you require it, not because I desire it." He shuttered his eyes.

"Do not just put your hand there. You must *try*, damn you," the King whispered fiercely. "You must really try."

Lancelot opened his eyes and some small fire, reflecting perhaps from the candles or the torches or the solstice flames, seemed to glow there for a moment. Then, in an instant, the fire in his eyes was gone. He stepped up to the stone, put his hand to the sword, and seemed to address it. His lips moved but no sound came out. Taking a deep breath, he pulled. Then, letting the breath out slowly, he leaned back.

The stone began to move.

The crowd gasped in a single voice.

"*Arthur . . .*" Kai began, his hand on the King's arm.

Sweat appeared on Lancelot's brow and the King could feel an answering band of sweat on his own. He could feel the weight of Lancelot's pull between his own shoulder blades and he held his breath with the knight.

The stone began to slide along the courtyard mosaic, but the sword did not slip from its mooring. It was a handle for the stone, nothing more. After a few inches, the stone stopped moving.

Lancelot withdrew his hand from the hilt, bowed slightly toward the King, and took two steps back.

"I cannot unsheath the King's sword," he said. His voice was remarkably level for a man who had just moved a ton of stone.

"Is there no one else?" asked Merlinnus, slowly looking around.

No one in the crowd dared to meet his eyes and there followed a long, full silence.

Then, from the left, came a familiar light voice. "Let King Arthur try." It was Gawen.

At once the crowd picked up its cue. "Arthur! Arthur! Arthur!" they shouted.

Wading into their noise like a swimmer in heavy swells breasting the waves, the King walked to the stone. Putting his right hand on the sword hilt, he turned his face to the people.

"For Britain!" he cried.

Merlinnus nodded, crossed his forefingers, and sighed a spell in Latin.

Arthur pulled. With a slight *whoosh* the sword slid out of the slot. He put his left hand above his right on the hilt and swung the sword over his head once, twice, and then a third time. Then he brought it slowly down before him until its point touched the earth.

"Now I be king. Of *all* Britain," he said.

Kai picked up the circlet from the stone and placed it on Arthur's head, and the chant of his name began anew. But even as he was swept up, up, up into the air by Kai and Lancelot, to ride their shoulders above the crowd, Arthur's eyes met the mage's. He whispered fiercely to Merlinnus, who could read his lips though his voice could scarcely carry against the noise.

"I will see you in your tower. Tonight!"

Merlinnus was waiting when, two hours later, the King slipped into his room, the sword in his left hand.

"So now you are king of all Britain indeed," said Merlinnus. "And none can say you no. Was I not right? A bit of legerdemain and . . ."

The king's face was grey in the room's candlelight.

"Merlinnus, you do not understand. I am *not* the king. There is another."

"Another what?" asked the mage.

"Another king. Another sword."

Merlinnus shook his head. "You are tired, lord. It has been a long day and an even longer night."

Arthur came over and grabbed the old man's shoulder with his right hand. "Merlinnus, *this is not the same sword.*"

"My lord, you are mistaken. It can be no other."

Arthur swept the small crown off his head and dropped it into the mage's lap. "I am a simple man, Merlinnus, and I am an honest one. I do not know much, though I am trying to learn more. I read slowly and understand only with help. What I am best at is soldiering. What I know best is swords. The sword I held months ago in my hands is not the sword I hold now. That sword had a balance to it, a grace such as I had never felt before. It knew me, knew my hand. There was a pattern on the blade that looked now like wind, now like fire. This blade, though it has fine watering, looks like nothing.

"I am not an imaginative man, Merlinnus, so I am not imagining this. This is not the sword that was in the stone. And if it is not, where is that sword? And what man took it? For he, not I, is the rightful-born king of all Britain. And I would be the first in the land to bend my knee to him."

Merlinnus put his hand to his head and stared at the crown in his lap. "I swear to you, Arthur, no man alive could move that sword from the stone lest I spoke the words."

There was a slight sound from behind the heavy curtains bordering the window, and a small figure emerged holding a sword in two hands.

"I am afraid that I took the sword, my lords."

"Gawen!" cried Merlinnus and Arthur at once.

The boy knelt before Arthur and held up the sword before him.

Arthur bent down and pulled the boy up. The sword was between them.

"It is I should kneel to you, my young king."

Gawen shook his head and a slight flush covered his cheeks. "I cannot be king now or ever. Not *rex quondam, rexque futurus.*"

"How pulled you the sword, then?" Merlinnus asked. "Speak. Be quick about it."

The boy placed the sword in Arthur's hands. "I brought a slab of butter to the stone one night and melted the butter over candle flames. When it was a river of gold I poured it into the slot and the sword slid out. Just like that."

"A trick. A homey trick that any herb wife might . . ." Merlinnus began.

Arthur turned on him, sadly. "No more a trick, mage, than my pulling a sword loosed by your spell. The boy is, in fact, the better of us two, for he worked it out by himself." He shifted and spoke directly to Gawen. "A king needs such cunning. But he needs a good right hand as well. I shall be yours, my lord, though I envy you the sword."

107

"The sword is yours, Arthur, never mine. Though I can now thrust and slash, having learned that much under the ham-handedness of your good tutor, I shall not ride to war. I have learned to fear the blade's edge as well as respect it." Gawen smiled.

The King turned again to Merlinnus. "Help me, mage. I do not understand."

Merlinnus rose and put the crown back on Arthur's head. "But I think I do, at last, though why I should be so slow to note it, I wonder. Age must dull the mind as well as the fingers. I have had an ague of the brain this fall. I said no man but you could pull the sword—and no *man* has." He held out his hand. "Come, child. You shall make a lovely May Queen, I think. By then the hair should be long enough for Sir Kai's list. Though what we shall ever do about the short utterances is beyond me."

"A *girl*? He's a girl?" Arthur looked baffled.

"Magic even beyond my making," said Merlinnus. "But what is your name, child? Surely not Gawen."

"Guenevere," she said. "I came to learn to be a knight in order to challenge Sir Gawain, who dishonored my sister. But I find—"

"That he is a bubblehead and not worth the effort?" interrupted Arthur. "He shall marry her *and* he shall be glad of it, for you shall be my queen and, married to your sister, he shall be my brother."

Guenevere laughed. "She will like that, too. Her head is as empty as his. But she *is* my sister. And she still loves him. Without a brother to champion her, I had to do."

Merlinnus laughed. "And you did splendidly. But about that butter trick . . ."

Guenevere put her hand over her breast. "I shall never tell as long as . . ." She hesitated.

"Anything," Arthur said. "Ask for anything."

"As long as I can have my sword back."

Arthur looked longingly at the sword, hefted it once, and then put it solemnly in her hand.

"Oh, not *this* one," Guenevere said. "It is too heavy and unwieldy. It does not sit well in my hand. I mean the other, the one that *you* pulled."

"Oh, *that*," said Arthur. "With all my heart."

I was browsing through Theda Kenyon's Witches Still Live, *a book published in 1931 and a great deal more interesting than its title would suggest, when I came upon the story of the farmer on Skye. At first I thought I was going to just retell the story in my own words, adding Scottish elements not given in the bare-bones outline she offered. But the story grew and changed. And while waiting for two of my cousins to arrive for a day of sightseeing, the ending suddenly came to me. Not what I expected at all.*

Trying stories on from different perspectives is always an interesting exercise. Like making the princess the villain in a story. I did that in my book Sleeping Ugly. *And in my story "The Thirteenth Fey." Here I have a family look at the witch story in Skye from several different angles until . . .*

McKinnon and McLeod are typical names from Skye.

Witchfinder

On the Isle of Skye lived a farmer named McKinnon whose cows suddenly gave no more milk.

"Bewitched they are!" he said, and went to discover the author of his misery.

He got himself a *buarach*, or bough of juniper, proof against witches, and bound it with horsehair to increase its power. Then he took himself and the stick off to Euart McLeod, a well-known witchfinder.

"Aye, and you have done this thing well," said McLeod, running a roughened hand over the buarach. "I canna find a thing wrong with it."

"Then will you say the words?" asked McKinnon.

"That I will," McLeod answered. And he did. He spoke for about half an hour over the "puir wee thing," the syllables rolling out like water over stone. And when he was done, he handed the buarach back to McKinnon, saying, "Fasten it to your barn and wait and see."

So McKinnon fastened it to his barn and he waited. He waited for day after day, till an entire week went by and the new moon rose, pale and thin as an old halfpenny.

One of the cows in the barn began to moan, a most unusual sound. And then the entire herd joined in. Then they muddled about till they broke loose of their ropes and in one terrifying rush shattered the barn door and scattered into the night.

Clattering down the road they went, with McKinnon fast behind. But it was no helter-skelter they were about. They were headed for one particular house. And when they got there, down went their heads and horns and they hooked and hacked at the walls.

The old woman who lived in the house came out with a stick and it was then McKinnon knew which witch had cursed his cows. He struck her dead on the spot and his cows gave milk ever after.

"What an awful story," Mother said, closing the book. "That poor old woman. And where was the justice in it?"

"Was she a witch?" Maddie was confused.

"No one said she was a witch," her mother pointed out. "Except for McKinnon. The cows were crazed, by the moon or by ill treatment. The house was probably the first they came to along the road. Possibly they were attracted to its thatched roof."

"It doesn't say that in the book," Jamie said. He was always the one who was a stickler for accuracy.

"No, it doesn't," his mother agreed. "But it is always important to read these old stories between the lines."

"What do you mean?" the children asked together.

She smiled gently at them. "It means there are different ways to look at the same story," she said. Her eyes closed and she got her story-telling expression on, which rarely happened during the day. "What if it went this way . . ."

111

On the Isle of Skye lived a nasty old skinflint named McKinnon who hoped that if he could get his cows to eat less and still give good milk he could make a greater profit. But as these things go, you get back what you put in. The less he fed them, the less milk his cows had. Until the day came when they gave none at all.

McKinnon was angry and he was cross, but he had a plan. He went to old Euart McLeod, a man known in some parts as a witch-finder and in some parts as crazy. "Find me the witch who made my cows dry up," said McKinnon, "and when they give milk again you will get a quart each week." It was an easy promise since he had no milk at all.

Well, McLeod wasn't as crazy as all that. He pulled his mumble and his jumble together. Then he took a stick of juniper and tied it with horsehair because that looked like a magical wand. And then, for good measure—because a quart of milk a week was worth it—he gave McKinnon a whole hour's worth of incantation made up on the spot. A bit of Bible and a bit of babble.

McKinnon went home well contented, let his cows out on the full moon as per McLeod's instructions, and followed them. They were so hungry they grazed along the roadside grass, though it was well into autumn and there was precious little to nibble on but brown stalks. And when they came to the very first thatched cottage along the road, they began to devour the thatch as well.

Now, the cottage belonged to Mistress Campbell, a woman not well liked because she came from off-island. She ran out, stick in hand, to drive the cows away, and McKinnon cried, "You are a witch." And he struck her dead with the juniper wand and took his cows home.

The cows were so full of fall grass and thatch that they gave milk for the first time in a month.

McLeod spoke for McKinnon at his trial and there was no one to speak up for the dead woman. She was judged a witch in truth and

112

since her land adjoined McKinnon's, he was given it by way of compensation, so he did not begrudge the milk to McLeod.

And everyone lived happily ever after.

"Everyone except the dead old woman," Jamie pointed out.

"Exactly," said his mother.

"That's not quite fair," Maddie complained, pulling on her left braid, something she did when disturbed. "You stacked the deck."

"That I did," her mother said. "Could you tell it better?"

Maddie thought a minute. Her left braid was quite straggled with her thinking and looked like a yellow haystack. But it wasn't often that she was positively invited to tell a story. Usually it was Jamie who got all the turns, as he was oldest and had the talent. "I think so," she said. "How about this?"

There was an old woman who lived on Skye who lots of people called a witch, but she wasn't. At least she didn't practice the dark arts. She was an herbalist. But she liked to keep herself to herself, which made them call her names even more.

Her next-door neighbor was a man with bad luck. He never did anything right. He would set in potatoes and they never grew, though *anyone* could grow them. He would plant corn and it would die. Even his cows stopped giving milk. His neighbors said he had been born under a thin star.

The old woman took pity on the man and showed him how to plant the proper way. She showed him how to nurse his cows so they gave milk again. All she asked in payment was a bit of milk for her tea.

At first the man was grateful. But then he grew tired of it. Gratitude can be a sour meal.

"No more milk for you, you old witch!" he said when she came to his door. He pushed her and she stumbled back and fell, her head hitting the foot of a juniper tree.

The man bent over and saw she was dead, and, panicking, ran to his brother-in-law for help.

The brother-in-law said, "Leave it to me." He stripped a bough from the tree, wound it with horsehair, and laid it by the woman's side. Then he called the town council to witness. "Look," he said, "the old woman was a witch. No wonder my poor brother-in-law had such ill luck."

So they buried the old woman by the crossroads with a stake in her heart and gave her land to the neighbor in compensation. And thus was justice—though it was wrong—served.

"Why, Maddie," her mother exclaimed, "I believe you do have the talent after all! You are just a late bloomer. That was a wonderful telling. Won't Gran be pleased!"

"Stakes and crossroads are for vampires," Jamie said in his careful way. "Not witches."

"How do you know?" Maddie asked.

"I read it in one of Gran's books."

They both turned to their mother for confirmation, and she nodded. "Witches were burned. Or thrown into the water. If they drowned, they were considered innocent," she said. "But if they floated, they were guilty. It was called 'swimming a witch.'"

"Fire . . ." Maddie said, and shuddered.

"And water," Jamie added. "What a combination."

For a moment all three were silent.

"Lucky it's not done anymore," Maddie said slowly, her hand once again on her left braid.

Jamie smiled. "At least we can swim on our own. You made us take lessons at the Y."

"Well, you were naturals," his mother said. "After all—witches can float." She got up and went over to the stove and stirred the pot carefully. "For starters."

I was at a full moon Wicca, or witchcraft, ceremony once, in a grove in California, when I was a speaker at a literature conference. There were no spells, no magic. The participants spoke of Mother Earth. They prayed that the connection between humanity and Earth should improve. Then they passed around the bounty of Her goodness—apple cider and chocolate-chip cookies.

This poem is about witches meeting under a succession of different trees. They invoke the names of goddesses like Astarte and Hecate, then mention the names of infamous witches. But when they meet under a rowan tree—the tree believed to be proof against witches—their meeting abruptly ends.

Witch Call

We were fifteen under the oak trees,
Call me Hecate, call me Astarte,
We were fifteen under the willows,
I am the witch's own.

We were fifteen under the chestnuts,
Call me Tituba, call me Wenham,
We were fifteen under the hornbeams,
I am the witch's own.

We were fifteen under the poplars,
Call me Samwell, call me Kyteler,
We were fifteen under the rowan—
Fly away . . . fly away . . . home.